The Cambridge Manuals of Science and Literature

BRASSES

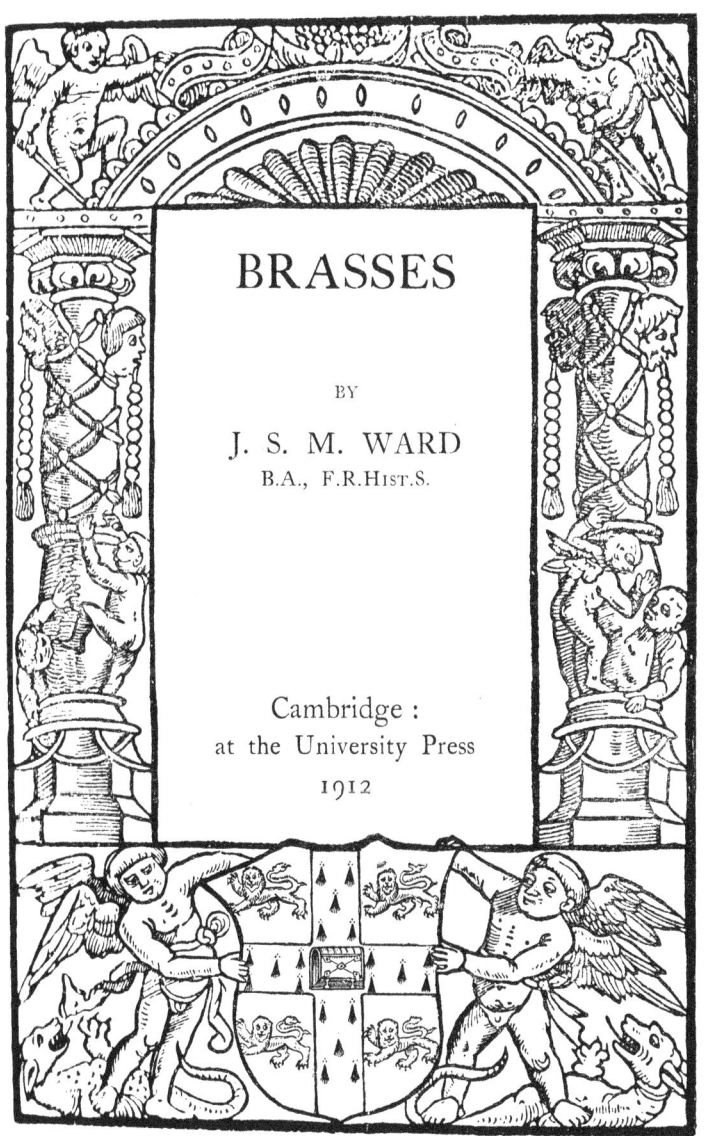

BRASSES

BY

J. S. M. WARD
B.A., F.R.Hist.S.

Cambridge:
at the University Press
1912

CAMBRIDGE UNIVERSITY PRESS
Cambridge, New York, Melbourne, Madrid, Cape Town,
Singapore, São Paulo, Delhi, Mexico City

Cambridge University Press
The Edinburgh Building, Cambridge CB2 8RU, UK

Published in the United States of America by Cambridge University Press, New York

www.cambridge.org
Information on this title: www.cambridge.org/9781107640900

© Cambridge University Press 1912

This publication is in copyright. Subject to statutory exception
and to the provisions of relevant collective licensing agreements,
no reproduction of any part may take place without the written
permission of Cambridge University Press.

First published 1912
First paperback edition 2012

A catalogue record for this publication is available from the British Library

ISBN 978-1-107-64090-0 Paperback

Cambridge University Press has no responsibility for the persistence or
accuracy of URLs for external or third-party internet websites referred to in
this publication, and does not guarantee that any content on such websites is,
or will remain, accurate or appropriate.

PREFACE

OF late years there has been a marked awakening of general interest in monumental brasses. Previously, the more imposing realism of statuary—either in single figures or in groups—may be said to have deprived these ancient relics of the recognition they deserved. But recently it has begun to dawn upon the more artistic members, at least of the thinking public, how much of real archaeological interest attaches to memorial brasses, hitherto known and appreciated only by the few.

As yet, however, there has been no cheap and handy manual which will give the ordinary man in the street a fair idea of the classes into which they may most readily be grouped, and at the same time furnish him with such essential details as will enable him to distinguish instinctively the salient points of the subject, and assimilate them to the full. It is hoped that this little volume will succeed in fulfilling this aim.

The arrangement of the chapters is into periods corresponding with those of History instead of the artificial method of grouping into *knights, knights and ladies, demi-figures,* etc. Those who would wish to follow up the subject in more extended form should read Mr Macklin's excellent work *The Brasses of England,* also Haines' *Manual* and Boutell's *Monumental Brasses.*

Most of the illustrations are from the author's own collection of rubbings (numbering over 1500), and practically all the letter-press and descriptions are based on his personal observations either from the rubbings or from the brasses themselves. In a few cases where this is not so, the author is indebted to one or other of those authors above mentioned. The Editor of *The Builder* has kindly given us permission for the use of two of the blocks made from the author's rubbings, which appeared in a recent number of that paper.

J. S. M. W.

August 16, 1912.

CONTENTS

CHAP.		PAGE
	Preface	v
I.	Edward I and II, 1272–1327	1
II.	Edward III and Richard II, 1328–99	9
III.	Lancastrian Period, 1400–53	14
IV.	The Yorkist Period, 1453–85	24
V.	Medieval Clergy	31
VI.	The Monasteries	43
VII.	The Early Tudors, 1485–1547	52
VIII.	Edward VI and Mary. Transitional Period	60
IX.	Elizabeth and James I, 1558–1625	62
X.	The Caroline Brasses, 1625–60	70
XI.	The Last Brasses, 1660–1773	75
XII.	Special Types	76
XIII.	Foreign Brasses	83
XIV.	Architectural Details	87
XV.	Conclusion	99
	Appendix	112
	Bibliography	148
	Index	149

LIST OF ILLUSTRATIONS

FIG.		PAGE
1.	Sir John Daubernon	2
2.	Sir John de Creke	4
3.	Sir John and Lady de Northwode	6
4.	Lady Joan de Cobham	7
5.	Sir Nicholas Burnell	11
6.	Margaret, Lady Cobham	13
7.	Thomas de Beauchamp, Earl of Warwick	16
8.	Sir Symon de Felbrigge and Margaret, his wife	18
9.	William Grevel and Wife	21
10.	Sir John Casey and Wife	23
11.	Sir William and Lady Vernon	26
12.	Sir Thomas Urswyk and family	29
13.	Laurence de St Maur	*at end*
14.	John Blodwell	*at end*
15.	Thomas Cranley, Archbishop of Dublin	41
16.	Thomas Neolond	45
17.	Eleanor de Bohun, Duchess of Gloucester	47
18.	John Shelley and Wife	54
19.	Lady Tiptoft	57
20.	Richard Wakehurst and Wife	59
21.	John Wingfield	65
22.	Alice, wife of William Wade	67
23.	Sir Edward Filmer and family	71
24.	John Strete	93
25.	Robert de Paris and Wife	95

CHAPTER I

EDWARD I AND II. 1272–1327

THE study of monumental brasses is one for which Englishmen have special opportunities, for in England there are more brasses than in all the other countries of Europe put together. The English brasses moreover differ curiously from those of the Continent. On the Continent the early engravers, probably influenced by the Limoges plates and incised slabs which preceded them, engraved figures, inscriptions and other details on rectangular plates. The monument of Geoffrey Plantagenet, 1150, father of Henry II of England, which is now in the Museum at Le Mans is such a plate. The enamelled effigy rests on a diapered background. The earliest brass is that of Bishop Iso von Wilpe, 1231, at Verden. (See Ch. XIII.)

In England, as the engravers copied the stone figures without backgrounds, they took the gravestone itself for the groundwork, and figures, canopies, inscriptions, etc. are each set into separate casements. The earliest *matrix* (at St Paul's, Bedford) shows a large Latin cross and is believed to commemorate Sir Simon de Beauchamp, 1208. The earliest *brass* now extant is that of 1277 at Stoke d'Abernon. To the first period belong in all twenty brasses (see Appendix).

The figure of Sir John Daubernon (1) shows the armour which had been worn for the last three centuries. He is in chain mail with *coif de mailles*, hawberk and *chausses* complete, but the junctions of these are not distinct. Single-pointed prickspurs are buckled round the ankles. The only sign of the coming change to plate armour are the *genouillères*, which protect the knees and are adorned with a fine pattern. They were probably at first made of leather, but later were of plate.

Over the mail is a linen surcoat, drawn tight round the waist by a cord. Suspended upon his left shoulder is his shield, small and heater-shaped, charged with his arms: *azure*, a *chevron or*. The ground of

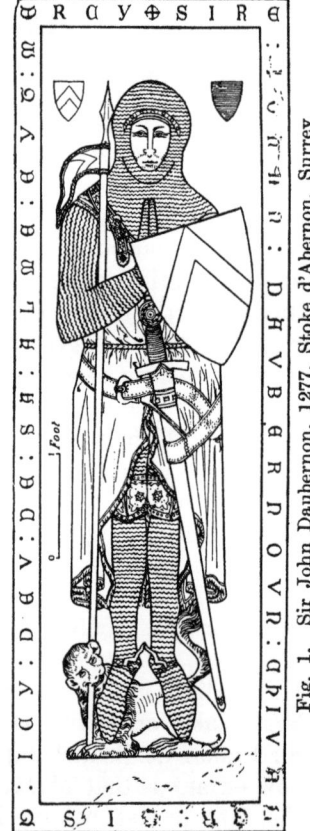

Fig. 1. Sir John Daubernon, 1277, Stoke d'Abernon, Surrey

I]   EDWARD I AND II, 1272–1327   3

the shield is in actual enamel—an almost unique feature. The cross-handled sword is attached to a broad belt and hangs in front of the body. This is the only brass which shows the lance. His feet rest on a lion, which is said to signify that he fell in battle.

Sir Roger de Trumpington differs from Sir John in several points. He has *ailettes* on his shoulders charged with his arms—three trumpets—and his shield is long instead of heater-shaped. Further, the great tilting helmet is placed under his head and is secured to his waist by a chain, and his legs are crossed. In 1270 he went on the Seventh Crusade with Prince Edward. So far as can be discovered, this is the only brass extant of a Crusader, but several other brasses of the same date have their legs crossed. This does not prove that they were Crusaders, but only that in some way they were benefactors to the Church.

Sir Richard de Boselyngthorpe (a demi-figure) wears gloves of fish-scale plates and holds a heart. Sir Robert de Bures is considered to be the finest military figure among all the brasses of England.

Sir Robert de Setvans is bare-headed and his gloves hang loosely from the wrists, leaving his hands bare. His arms (winnowing fans, hence the name Setvans) are shown on his surcoat, *ailettes*, and long shield. Both he and Sir Robert de Bures are cross-legged. There is probably French influence in this brass.

Next follow two transitional figures at Pebmarsh and Gorleston. Both originally had canopies, which have now entirely disappeared. In these the outsides of the upper and forearms are protected by steel plates strapped over the mail, small elbow-pieces are added, and round plates are fixed in front of the shoulders and at the bend of the arms. Shin plates may also be noticed.

Sir John de Creke is a fair example of a fourteenth century knight clad almost entirely in plate-armour, for we now pass definitely to the second type of armour known as the "cyclas." This garment is shown in the illustration and is also depicted in the brass of Sir John Daubernon II. It takes the place of the surcoat, is slit up the sides, and is shorter in front than behind.

It therefore shows beneath, first the gambeson, then the hawberk of mail, and, finally, the padded haqueton. The hands are bare and the hawberk sleeves short, thus showing the forearms entirely protected by vambraces of plate worn under, not over, the mail. The upper arms have pieces of

Fig. 2.
Sir John de Creke, c. 1325, Westley Waterless, Cambs.

plate over the chain, as before. A steel bascinet is on the head, and the quatrefoil device on its apex was probably meant to hold a crest or a lady's favour.

Sir John (II) has the earliest ogee-arch canopy. There was a fine double one at Westley Waterless, but not a vestige of it remains.

Sir John de Northwode's effigy is almost certainly the work of a French craftsman. His shield hangs at his left hip instead of on his arm, which was a very usual method in France. The style of the engraving, too, points in the same direction. His helmet is secured by a chain, his head rests on a pillow and his forearms are protected by scale-armour. About 1510, the lower portion of the figure having been lost, new legs were engraved. Though an effort has been made to preserve the style of 1330, yet the new work is obviously Tudor. The altered shape of the feet and badly depicted lion readily show this. At the same time, a strip was cut out of the middle to make the knight of the same length as his wife! This removed the arm of the cross in his shield, as shown in the illustration, but the missing piece has recently been restored.

We must now consider the costume of the ladies, of whom the first is Margarete de Camoys, c. 1310. There was originally a canopy of the earlier, or straight-sided type, and a border inscription in Lombardic letters. Further, there were eight shields and thirty-one stars or other devices on the slab. The figure alone

Fig. 3. Sir John and Lady de Northwode,
c. 1330, Minster-in-Sheppey, Kent

EDWARD I AND II, 1272–1327

survives and has on it nine blank shields, probably the matrices of shields of enamel.

Joan de Cobham, c. 1320, is the next lady. Her straight-sided canopy is the only survivor of this early type. She wears a loose-fitting robe with short sleeves, below which can be seen the sleeves of her kirtle. Her head and neck are covered with a veil and wimple.

Lady de Creke wears a long mantle fastened across the breast by a cord and gathered up under the arm. The mark of the engraver is at her foot. This is almost unique.

Lady de Northwode has a mantle with side openings, through which the arms pass. It is turned back in front to show the lining of variegated fur. The head

Fig. 4. Lady Joan de Cobham, c. 1320, Cobham, Kent

is bare and the hair plaited; a stiff wimple covers the neck. Her head rests on a handsome cushion.

Maud de Bladigdone has a dress similar to Joan de Cobham's.

She and her husband are small demi-figures in the centre of an octofoil cross, most of which had to be restored in 1887. He wears a tunic buttoned down the front, with tight sleeves having long lappets from the elbows and a tippet over his shoulders. His beard is small and forked.

The remaining brasses are to priests in mass vestments, excepting Archbishop Wm. de Grenefeld. But we shall deal with the vestments of the clergy in a separate chapter.

The Chinnor, Merton College and Woodchurch brasses are in varying forms of crosses. Chinnor has only the head in the centre, Merton a fine demi-figure, and Woodchurch a small figure. Until 1857 there existed a fine, large brass to a priest Adam de Bacon (1310), at Oulton in Suffolk. Unfortunately in that year it was stolen (and probably melted down). The two remaining priests are simple demi-figures.

There was originally a fine canopy over Archbishop Grenefeld with side shafts containing saints. All this has long since perished and 18 inches of the lower portion of the figure were stolen in 1829.

These early figures all have very curly hair.

CHAPTER II

BRASSES DURING THE REIGNS OF EDWARD III AND RICHARD II

WE now find brasses commemorating members of almost every class, but the first to claim our attention will be the military ones.

A small group of three transitional but mutilated brasses must be taken first:

Of these that of Sir Hugh Hastings (1347) at Elsing, in Norfolk, is the most interesting. His legs are now missing, but from an old rubbing in the British Museum we know they were enclosed in chain mail. The cyclas, worn shorter than hitherto, only reaches to the middle of the thighs. Upon it is the maunche or sleeve of the Hastings family, richly diapered, and differenced with a label of three points. This also appears on his small heater-shaped shield. A belt hangs over his hips with the sword on the left side, fastened in front. A hawberk of mail was worn beneath the cyclas and the haqueton shows at the wrists. A bascinet protects his head and a gorget of plate encircles his neck. Additional plates are attached to the arms, and roundels are placed at the elbows and below the shoulders. Cuisses of pourpoint appear for the first time upon the thighs. These were of leather (*cuir-bouilli*) studded with small steel plates.

The canopy (now much mutilated) is very fine. Originally there were four canopied niches on either side with "weepers," or mourners, in the military costume of the day. Three were missing, though of these one, Lord Grey de Ruthyn, was preserved at the Fitzwilliam Museum, Cambridge, and has lately, we believe, been restored to its place. Those left are: Top dexter side, Edward III crowned, with the arms of England and France on his cyclas. Below him, Thos. de Beauchamp, holding a lance. Top sinister side, the Earl of Lancaster—Henry Plantagenet, the next is lost, then Lord Stafford, and then Almeric, Lord St Armand, who wears a ridged steel hat with a broad rim over his bascinet, which is almost unique.

Within a circle in the arch of the canopy is St George, and beneath him the soul is being borne upwards by two angels.

There are several other interesting details which it would take too long to describe. The brass at Wimbish, in Essex (1347), consists of a much mutilated cross, which contains within its head Sir John de Wantone and his lady. He greatly resembles Sir Hugh, save that his legs are partly clad in plate, as in the de Creke brass.

Sir John Giffard (1348) at Bowers Gifford in

Essex, has a suit of banded chain with very few pieces of plate, and at first sight might be considered a reversion to the type of Sir John Daubernon I, but a closer inspection will show that his linen cloak is much more like the jupon, which was destined very soon to take the place of the cyclas. The head is lost. The Giffard coat of arms (six *fleurs-de-lys*) is displayed on his shield.

The Hundred Years' War caused a development of armour which lasted practically unaltered for fifty years.

The type is clearly depicted in the illustration of Sir Nicholas Burnell, 1382, Acton Burnell, Shropshire. The hawberk of mail has shrunk to a vest and shows only at the arm-pits and lower edge. A cuirass of

Fig. 5. Sir Nicholas Burnell, 1382, Acton Burnell, Salop

steel covers this and has over it a leather jupon, which is often ornamented with its owner's coat-of-arms. The Burnell brass here illustrated shows the armour of this type. The sharply-pointed bascinet is connected with the body armour by a camail of chain, hence this style of armour is often called the *camail style*. The arms and legs are entirely enclosed in plate in the later examples, but in the earlier cuirasses of pourpoint are used for the thighs, as in the brass of Sir John de Cobham, 1365. A bawdric, or broad belt, worn straight round the hips, held on the right a misericorde (dagger) and on the left a sword.

The dress of ladies of this period consists usually of a close-fitting kirtle, buttoned tightly from neck to waist and from elbow to wrist, and sometimes right down the front. Over this is worn a mantle, open in front, and kept in position by a cord across the breast, see illustration.

Sometimes a third dress appears (with or without the mantle) over the kirtle. It has two forms, one very like the kirtle, but with close-fitting sleeves cut short at the elbow, with long lappets; the other form is the sideless *cote-hardi*. This is slit up at the sides and edged with fur at the openings. It has no sleeves or sides as far as the hips.

The first form is seen at Gt. Berkhampstead, Herts., 1356, Bray, Berks., 1378, and elsewhere. The second

EDWARD III AND RICHARD II

is found at Lingfield, Surrey, c. 1370, and Cobham, Kent, 1375.

A long overcoat sometimes takes the place of the mantle, as at Chinnor, Oxford, c. 1385. The hair is usually enclosed in a net and plaited. Mittens are often worn. Widows wear a veil with a barbe and wimple and are often hard to distinguish from Vowesses, i.e. ladies who at the death of their husbands take the vows in a nunnery.

Alianore de Bohun, Duchess of Gloucester (1399), being a vowess, is illustrated in the chapter dealing with the religious orders. With its triple canopy it is one of the most splendid brasses still existing.

The Cobham brasses especially should be noticed. This church has the most magnificent series extant

Fig. 6. Margaret, Lady Cobham, 1395, Cobham, Kent

anywhere. They number 19 and most of them have fine canopies. A visit to this little village is therefore well repaid.

We must now turn to the civilians. These are often of considerable interest.

By far the finest is the mutilated brass of Walter Pescod. He lies beneath a fine canopy and supercanopy, and further reference will be made to this in the chapter on architectural detail. He wears a close-fitting tunic buttoned down the front, and a mantle with a hood. In the small demi-figures the mantle is usually omitted.

Frankelins wore a tunic, hood, and mantle buttoned over the right shoulder. From the girdle hung an anlace, or short sword. This dress can be seen at King's Somborne, Felbrigg and Wimington. Beards are usually, though not always, worn. Richard Torrington's feet rest on a lion, as if he were a knight, but this is unusual. (See list.)

CHAPTER III

LANCASTRIAN PERIOD. 1400–1453

THERE now begins to be evident a slight deterioration; careless and poor work is found side by side with some of the very finest. In part this is

III] LANCASTRIAN PERIOD, 1400-53 15

because so many different classes were now adopting this type of monument.

About 500 brasses belong to this period, including clergy and laity.

The armed figures may be conveniently divided into three groups, and it will be found that their wives naturally fall into similar divisions.

The first is practically the same as that of the later Plantagenets and still retains the camail. (See list (I).)

Sir Wm. Bagot and his wife wear the collar of S. S. This collar was conferred by Henry IV and the other Lancastrians on their friends. It is found on many brasses during this period and is worn by ladies as well as knights. We may appropriately refer here to the Order of the Garter. Unfortunately there are not many instances of its being shown on brasses, only six or seven being known. (See Appendix.)

Our illustration of Thomas de Beauchamp, Earl of Warwick, not only shows the style of armour, but also that the armorial charges on his jupon and on his wife's mantle are wrought with a beautiful diaper work. This way of depicting arms (by lightly engraving the surface with dots, instead of lines) is unique.

The ladies in this division, like their husbands, wear practically the same costume as before. But at the same time other brasses were being laid down

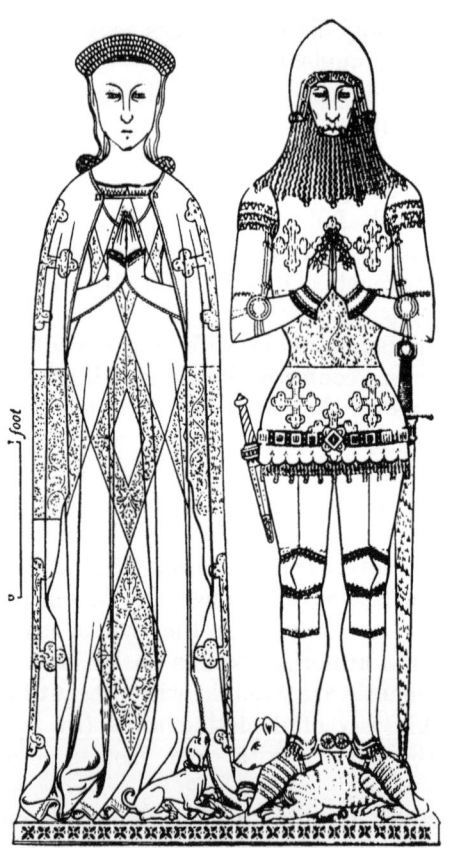

Fig. 7. Thomas de Beauchamp, Earl of Warwick, 1401, St Mary's, Warwick

III] LANCASTRIAN PERIOD, 1400–53 17

showing that changes were taking place. The jupon was abandoned, and the plain cuirass shown. This has a skirt of hoops, known as taces. These cover the mail shirt, which gradually disappears. The camail is likewise covered by a gorget of steel and later abandoned. The bascinet becomes globular.

An interesting example of the transitional period is the brass of Sir Thos. Swynborne and his father at Little Horkesley in Essex. The father, Sir Robert (died 1391), is shown in the armour of that date, while his son shows the armour of 1412.

Later, roundels are placed at the elbow and in front of the armpits. (See list (II).)

The illustration of Sir Simon Felbrigge is of special interest. He holds the Royal Standard in his right hand charged with the arms of Edward the Confessor impaling France and England. He was the Royal Standard bearer during Richard II's reign, yet was made K.G. by Henry V. He did not die till 1443, but probably prepared his tomb in 1416. The palettes at his armpits are charged with the cross of St George, and he wears the Garter. Additional plates are placed on the shoulders and cuirass. More changes now occur, the left side begins to be more fully protected than the right, since the extra weight would have prevented free action. Tuilles or plates are strapped to the lowest tace, and other slight changes become noticeable.

18 BRASSES [CH.

Fig. 8. Sir Symon de Felbrigge, K.G., and Margaret, his wife, 1416, Felbrigg, Norfolk

III] LANCASTRIAN PERIOD, 1400–53 19

For examples of these changes see list (III) in the Appendix.

Sir Christopher Baynham (c. 1448) at Newland, Gloucester, has a most curious crest—a miner with a candle in his mouth, a bag on his back and a pick-axe in his hand. The brass is unfortunately rather mutilated.

In the last section (section (iv)) the helmet is discarded and the hair is close-cropped. The skirt of taces is very long, having often ten hoops; tuilles are not used. Pauldrons are worn on the shoulders.

The ladies do not vary in costume so much. The mantle is often omitted and a high-waisted gown with long sleeves and turned-down collar worn. The hair is gathered into a net and a kerchief draped over the top.

Examples may be found at Routh, Yorks., c. 1410; East Markham, Notts., 1419; Digswell, Herts., 1415; Horley, Surrey (canopy), c. 1420.

From 1420–1450 we find the plain kirtle and mantle (occasionally the sideless *cote-hardi*, as at Trotton) and the horned or mitred head-dress. This means that the hair, enclosed in a net, is raised above the head in the design indicated and then draped with a kerchief. Most of the ladies depicted with their husbands follow this arrangement.

Examples alone, at Hever, Kent, 1419; Lingfield, Surrey, 1420; Cobham, Kent, 1433, etc.

The civilians are of great importance during this period, and two groups demand special attention, the Woolmen and the Judges. Wm. Grevel and wife, Chipping Campden, Glos., 1401 (woolman) may be taken as an example of the earlier type. He wears a long gown buttoned right down the front, a belt with an anlace, and mantle opening at the right shoulder. His wife has no mantle and wears a similar dress to that of the Plantagenet period. The magnificent double canopy has a central column, a rare feature.

This type of dress, with slight variations, continued for the whole of the Lancastrian period. Towards its close, however, certain changes became more and more common. Mantle and hood are seldom seen, except as a sign of municipal office. The dress becomes shorter, reaching only a little below the knees, the hair is cropped and there is no beard. Nicholas Canteys, St John's, Margate, 1431, is an exception, having a long beard.

The brasses of the woolmen are the finest, as they were the richest. Their feet often rest upon woolpacks or lambs.

In many brasses, merchants' marks on shields will be found, as in Grevel's. At Fletching, Sussex, there is a curious brass to Peter Denot, glover, 1450. It consists of a pair of gloves and an inscription.

The fine series of woolmen's brasses at Northleach

III] LANCASTRIAN PERIOD, 1400–53 21

Fig. 9. William Grevel (woolman) and wife, 1401, Chipping Campden, Glos.

are specially noticeable, and Gloucestershire takes the lead throughout England, Lincolnshire coming next.

We cannot leave the subject of the civilians without referring to the legal profession. The judges are by far the most important. (See Appendix.)

John Cottusmore and his wife (1439) have two brasses; the first large, with a fine canopy on the floor, the second small, on the wall, showing them kneeling.

The costume consists of a gown reaching to the feet, with close sleeves. A fur tippet, a mantle lined with minever, a hood and a close cap or coif.

Sir John Cassy, chief baron of the Exchequer (1400), has a magnificent brass at Deerhurst. He shows most of these features but the tippet, which is concealed. The fine double canopy no longer has the figure of St John the Baptist, which was still there when the rubbing was taken. The other figure is of St Anne and the Virgin as a child. The inscription, as is often the case in Gloucestershire, is in raised letters with curious leaves, and a dragon separating the words, but the lower part is here omitted. The dog beneath Lady Cassy's feet was evidently meant to represent an old pet. It has a collar of bells round its neck and its name, Terri, underneath. This is the only named pet now extant, but a "Jakke" existed formerly at Ingham, Norfolk,

Fig. 10. Sir John Casey and wife (part of marginal inscription omitted), 1400, Deerhurst, Glos.

on the brass of Sir Bryan de Stapleton, 1438. It was sold as old metal in 1800.

Three Serjeants-at-law belong to this period: John Rede, Checkendon, Oxon. (triple canopy), 1404, Nich. Roland and wife, Cople, Beds., c. 1410, and Thos. Rolf, Gosfield, Essex, 1439.

Thomas Rolf has the most characteristic dress, consisting of a cassock and academical tabard, a tippet, hood with two bands and a coif.

These include most types of civilian brasses, but there are numerous variations, and therein lies the interest of the subject.

CHAPTER IV

THE YORKIST PERIOD. 1453–1485

DURING the Wars of the Roses, England was practically isolated from the Continent. It is therefore not surprising that this period has a character of its own.

There are about 350 brasses, and these include an entirely distinct type of armour and a characteristic female head-dress.

There are not many really fine brasses, canopies are few and heavy in design, and the engraving is poor. The proportions are often bad. In particular the head is often made too big or too small.

IV] THE YORKIST PERIOD, 1453-85 25

The great characteristic of the armour of this period is the addition of extra pieces of huge size and curious shape. Yet all were the outcome of the exigencies of the time. So too were the ridges and flutings which were meant to deflect the point of a weapon. The armour was also decorated with punching, engraving, etc.

During the wars in France, the knights had often dismounted and fought on foot. During the Wars of the Roses, they usually charged on horseback. This explains why the heavier armour is on the upper part of the body, while the lower is more lightly protected.

Often the upper half therefore seems out of proportion.

Usually the head is bare, but occasionally the "sallad" or shell helmet is found, as at Castle Donington, Cirencester, Addington, Sprotborough and elsewhere. Among other peculiarities, a hooked lance-rest is often screwed to the right side of the cuirass, as at Hildersham. The elbow-pieces often attain to an enormous size. The tuilles have been re-introduced. The shoes are long and pointed, the sword slung in front.

The illustration of Sir Wm. and Lady Vernon, Tong, Salop, 1467, betrays one of the signs of deterioration: the head rests on the helmet with crest, yet the figure *stands* on a field of grass. His wife wears

Fig. 11. Sir William and Lady Vernon, 1467, Tong, Salop

THE YORKIST PERIOD, 1453-85

kirtle, sideless *cote-hardi*, mantle, veil and the widow's wimple. Her feet rest against an extraordinary dragon. This is probably in allusion to her name and patron saint, Margaret, whose emblem was a dragon.

In the Morley brass (1470) the knight rests his head on his helmet and stands on grass and flowers. The two wives wear the mitre head-dress and there are three saints above. These are St Christopher, St Anne and the Virgin, and St Mary and Child.

During this period, armorial tabards and heraldic kirtles and mantles became common.

The earliest tabard is at Amberley, Sussex, 1424.

Examples during the Yorkist period are found as follows: Wm. Stapilton and wife, Edenhall, Cumberland, 1458; Hen. Grene and wife, Lowick, Northants., 1467; Sir Jn. Say and wife, Broxbourne, Herts., 1473; Sir Thos. Sellynger and wife, St George's Chapel, Windsor, 1475; Philip Mede and two wives, St Mary, Redcliff, Bristol, 1475.

The Yorkist collar of stars and roses takes the place of the S.S. It is found at Broxbourne, St Albans, Little Easton, 1483, and elsewhere.

The horned head-dress of the ladies changes to the mitred, as at Thornton and Morley. The memorial of Ly. Joyce Tiptoft, Enfield, Middlesex, c. 1470, is one of the few really fine brasses of the period and shows the dress and armorial bearings well. The canopy is fine, possibly copied from that of the Duchess of Gloucester (1399) in Westminster Abbey. The arrangement of shields hung from the shafts of the canopy is only one of several similar features. The head is far too large, as is often the case at this date, and spoils the general effect. Her jewelled necklace should be noticed (page 57).

The butterfly head-dress begins to replace the mitred head-dress, hitherto in vogue. A veil of gauze was extended over wires. In real life it was doubtless light and beautiful, but in brass it looks heavy and ungainly. The wife of Sir Thos. Urswyk, Dagenham, Essex, shows this type of *coiffure*. She also wears a low-necked gown, showing the upper part of the corsage. Her cuffs and necklace are characteristic, and her somewhat awkward poise is typical of the period. Her daughters are of special interest. The head-dresses of the six younger are formed by conical nets of several designs, their long hair hanging down behind. These examples are unique. The eldest daughter is a nun, and the other two resemble their mother, but wear no mantle. The sons wore the ordinary civilian costume of the time, but have quite recently been stolen.

Widows still wear the wimple, and maidens have long, flowing hair.

There is but little variety in the dress of civilians. The anlace becomes rare and its place is often taken

IV] THE YORKIST PERIOD, 1453-85 29

Fig. 12. Sir Thomas Urswyk and family, 1479, Dagenham, Essex

by a rosary. The hair is close-cropped, and the figures usually small. Mantles are only worn as a sign of office.

The *Woolmen* and the *Lawyers* represent the best work to be seen at this epoch. Of the latter, Sir Thos. Urswyk, 1479, Chief Baron of the Exchequer, already mentioned, will serve as an example. He is bareheaded, and the fur lining of his mantle is visible, as is his rosary. His sons display the usual costume of the day without the mantle.

Notaries wear a plain gown with pencase and inkhorn hanging from the belt. A scarf and a cap are fastened on the left shoulder. (Appendix.)

We have now come to the close of the Middle Ages. The signs of deterioration of this, as of other medieval arts, are apparent.

The question may be asked—In what language and type were the inscriptions engraved? Briefly, the earlier (in Norman French) are engraved in separated Lombardic letters which were inserted round the edge of the slab. This gave place to a border fillet. This fillet soon began to be engraved in Gothic characters. In the fifteenth century Latin became the usual language—from the beginning it had been used for *ecclesiastics*. It never entirely fell out of use, but towards the end of the fifteenth century English began to appear. During the sixteenth and seventeenth centuries the

IV] THE YORKIST PERIOD, 1453–85 31

latter takes the place of Latin to a large extent. Roman characters replaced Gothic in the seventeenth century.

The arbitrary contractions of words employed by the engravers from the earliest to the latest periods render the deciphering of a large proportion of the inscriptions no easy task.

CHAPTER V

MEDIEVAL CLERGY

Deacons.

THERE is no complete brass to a deacon now extant, and there exists but one solitary mutilated example at Burwell, Cambridge, on the reverse of part of the brass of John Lawrence, Abbot of Ramsey.

The dalmatic was their distinguishing vestment. It was shorter than an alb, slit up on either side for a short distance and had a straight edge before and behind. The left side and lower edge were fringed for a deacon, *both* sides when worn by a bishop.

When St Stephen, St Philip or St Lawrence appear in canopies, they wear this vestment.

The tunicle was worn by sub-deacons. It is similar to the dalmatic, but of linen, whereas the latter was usually of silk and often richly decorated.

Mass Vestments.

The most numerous brasses to the clergy are to the incumbents of our country churches, and these are usually depicted in mass vestments. The average country parson was, as now, a man of modest means, and so it is not surprising that these brasses as a rule are small, and very few have canopies or even marginal inscriptions. There is but little development in any of the vestments, as these had become fixed in their main features many centuries earlier.

The chief characteristic change is that the hair of early ecclesiastics is long and curly and tends to become less so, till by Tudor times it is absolutely straight. In fourteenth century brasses the material of the vestments seems to be thin and fits closely to the body, whereas later it is stiff and heavy.

The fylfot cross is found on the vestments of many priests, as at Kemsing, Kent, c. 1320, and in the brass of Rich. de Hakebourne, Merton College, Oxford, 1310. This ancient symbol, known in the Sanscrit as the *swastika*, is found on Buddhist inscriptions in India and China, on Greek vases and Roman pavements (as at Brading, I.o.W.) and on Runic inscriptions and elsewhere. On brasses it is mainly found upon those of the fourteenth century.

We will consider in detail the monument of Lawrence de St Maur, 1337, at Higham Ferrers, which must serve for all the others (see frontispiece). It is by far the finest, and, indeed, there are only four or five others with canopies at all, and hardly a dozen have effigies over three feet long. The central panel of the canopy contains God the Father, the soul and two angels, St Peter and St Paul, St Andrew and St Thomas. At the four corners are the Evangelists. Then, St Gabriel opposite (perhaps) St Mary; St John Baptist opposite (perhaps) the Magdalene; St Stephen opposite (perhaps) St Lawrence; the Abbot St Maur opposite St Christopher, whose bare feet can be seen standing in a river. Beneath the priest's feet are two dogs quarrelling over a bone.

The total length of the brass is 8 ft. 3 inches, and breadth 3 ft. 5 inches.

The figure wears an *alb* with apparels at the foot and on each arm. In the earliest brasses these pieces of embroidery went right round the wrists, but they were soon reduced to simple squares. The amice encircles the neck and is like a handkerchief with a strip of embroidery along one side. As worn it looks like a collar. The stole was crossed over the breast and held in place by the girdle of the alb. Usually, as here, only the ends can be seen. At Sudborough, Northants., 1415, at Horsham, Sussex, c. 1430, and at Upwell, Norfolk, 1435, it can be seen in entirety. Over the left arm hangs the maniple, a strip of embroidery, similar to a stole. Over all he wears a fine chasuble. In this case there is a narrow band of embroidery round the edge, but this is unusual. The ordinary type is perfectly plain. In the sixteenth century a central pillar of embroidery or orphrey is common. It is also found on the chasubles of bishops and abbots at an earlier date. Occasionally, the whole ground was covered with a pattern.

It will be noticed that many priests are represented holding chalices. There is quite a considerable group of brasses consisting of chalices only. They all commemorate priests. The selected list in the Appendix will be useful to those who wish to study them more closely. It was customary to bury pewter chalices with priests who were interred in their mass vestments. The author himself has one of these coffin chalices. It was probably from this custom that the idea originated of making chalice brasses. The earliest are in Yorkshire; there are many in Norfolk, but few outside these counties.

Robt. Wodehowse's brass at Holwell, Beds., 1515, has as a rebus two wode-howses, or wild men, with clubs, on either side of the chalice.

There is a peculiar brass at Winwick, Lancashire, to Sir Peter Legh, 1527. On the death of his wife, he gave up his calling as a knight and became a priest.

He is bare-headed and has a tonsure. Over his

armour he wears a chasuble, and between his hands is a coat-of-arms.

CHOIR AND PROCESSIONAL VESTMENTS

The Almuce.

Except when at Mass, the usual vestments worn were cassock and surplice, almuce, hood and cope.

The cassock was the ordinary walking dress of the clergy. In a few cases it is shown alone. (Appendix.)

The almuce was a large cape turned down over the shoulders and lined with fur. D.D.'s and canons wore one lined with grey fur, and the former had the outside cloth scarlet.

All others wore dark-brown fur. The tails of the animals were sewn round the edge and two long lappets hung down in front. The fur lining is the only part shown in brasses, and this is usually represented by cutting away the metal and filling up the surface with lead or coloured earths. Of these there are a fair number. (Appendix.)

The Cope.

More usually the *cope* accompanies the almuce. Over a hundred brasses of coped priests remain. Many are both large and fine, with canopies. They usually commemorate Church dignitaries.

The cope was a beautiful and costly vestment,

shaped like a cloak, and was fastened across the breast by the morse. Orphreys adorned the straight edges. The general surface was usually plain, though occasionally covered by a pattern, as in the case of Robt. Langton, Queen's College, Oxford, 1518, and John White, Winchester College, Hants., c. 1548. This is generally a sign of late work. A small, semicircular hood attached to the back of the cope was usually hidden by the upper part of the almuce, the lappets of which are also visible beyond the long sleeves of the surplice.

The two following are among the finest extant:

John Sleford, Balsham, Cambs., 1401, was Rector of Balsham, Master of the Wardrobe to Edward III, Chaplain to Queen Philippa, Canon of Wells and later of Ripon, Archdeacon of Wells, etc. The whole composition measures $8\frac{1}{2}$ ft. × $4\frac{1}{2}$ ft., and the figure is 5 ft. 2 in. long. The triple canopy supports a shrine which is divided in half. The lower portion shows the soul of the deceased supported in a sheet by two angels. He is being borne up to the Holy Trinity, who are represented in the upper story. Two seraphim are poised on the finials of the two side arches.

The shields are: dexter, quarterly Old France and England; sinister, the same impailing Hainault. The arms of the See of Ely (three crowns) are shown on the third shield, and the fourth is lost.

v] MEDIEVAL CLERGY 37

Down the orphreys of the cope are depicted five pairs of saints under embattled canopies: St Mary and St John Baptist; St John the Evangelist and St Etheldreda; St Catherine and St Peter; St Paul and St Margaret; St Mary Magdalene and St Wilfred. The sacred monogram I. S. is shown on the morse and also on two roundels.

The other brass is equally fine and measures 8 ft. 9 in. × 4 ft. 1 in.

John Blodwell was Dean of St Asaph, Prebend of Lichfield and of Hereford, Canon of St David's and Rector of Balsham. His canopy is of a different type to Sleford's. It has a single arch resting on broad shafts, in each of which are four niches with saints. The cope has saints down the orphreys which are rather worn. The whole surface is adorned with lions' heads. The inscription is in a dialogue between Blodwell and his guardian angel. The Dean's words are in relief.

The alb and amice are substituted for surplice and almuce at Horsham, 1411, Upwell, 1428 and 1435, Beeford, Yorks., 1472, Hitchin, 1498, and Rauceby, 1536.

Canons of Windsor, instead of a cope, wore the mantle of the Order of the Garter. It has a small cross on the left shoulder and is found on the brasses of Roger Parker (headless demi), Northstroke, Oxon., 1370; Unknown, Bennington, Herts. (mutilated, an ordinary cope with badge on shoulder), c. 1450; Roger Lupton, Eton College, 1540; Arthur Cole, Magdalen College, Oxford, 1558.

Academic Dress.

There are a considerable number of brasses showing the academic dress, in all 75 to 80.

About one-third are at Oxford and Cambridge, and the rest are widely scattered. The distinction between the various degrees being usually made by the colour and material rather than by the shape renders the task of differentiating difficult.

The academic tabard without sleeves, the cape or tippet, and the hood are usually worn over a cassock, as on the brasses of Thos. Mason, M.A., of Magdalen, Oxford, 1501, and of John London, M.A., S.T.P., of New College, Oxford, 1508. Sometimes the academic tabard has short sleeves.

The taberdium talare is longer and probably implies a B.D., though it is worn by others who had not this degree. Good examples are to be seen on the brasses of John Bloxham, B.D., Merton College, Oxford, c. 1420 (with John Whytton on bracket) (see Chap. XIV), and of Wm. Blakwey, Little Wilbraham, Cambs (kn.), 1521.

D.D.'s have the *cappa clausa*. This is a plain, sleeveless gown, and the arms appear through a single opening, which only reaches to the waist.

MEDIEVAL CLERGY

The tippet is usually of fur, and a cap is worn. The latter is either a skull cap or raised one or two inches and brought to a low point in the centre. The first type is shown in the brass of Dr Billingford, St Benet's, Cambridge, 1432; the second in the brass of Dr Towne, at King's College, Cambridge, 1496.

Doctors of other faculties wear the cap and pallium, a long gown similar to the taberdium talare. It must not be confounded with the pallium of an archbishop. Many academic persons wear the cope or almuce, sometimes with the doctor's cap. There are a few academic brasses of Elizabethan and Jacobean date. They usually show the long, civilian gown of the period. From it has developed the present University gown, which has not sprung from the ancient tabard.

Bishops.

Bishops and Mitred Abbots wore the mass vestments of the priests with certain additions. The tunicle and dalmatic were worn below the chasuble. The former is often of the same length as the dalmatic and so cannot bè seen. Sandals adorned with jewels and gloves similarly ornamented were usually worn. The episcopal ring had a single precious stone.

The mitre and crozier are perhaps the most characteristic vestments. The earliest mitres were low with plain edges; they gradually became higher and crockets were added to the sides of the horns. In brasses the extreme height to which they developed is not shown. They were made of plain linen, of embroidered linen and of precious metals. Two narrow strips of silk called "infulae" hung down from the back of the mitre. These can be seen in the brasses at York and East Horsley.

The crozier and pastoral staff are the same, the cross staff of the archbishop is not really a crozier at all. The latter represents the shepherd's crook. A scarf was often fastened to the knob below the crook. It was called either an "infula"—like the ribbons of a mitre—or "vexillum." The latter name refers to the Cross banner of Constantine.

Croziers and mitres are depicted long after vestments had fallen into disuse. The last crozier, 1631, is at Chigwell, Essex. Mitres are found even later, but are probably used as a crest.

Archbishops generally hold the cross staff instead of a crozier and wear the *pall*. It was simply a narrow loop of white lamb's wool placed round the neck and with a weighted band hanging down before and behind.

Thos. Cranley, 1417, clearly shows all the vestments; his cross, as was often the case, was a crucifix. The triple canopy with super-canopy is exceptionally fine, though somewhat mutilated.

Fig. 15. Thomas Cranley, Archbishop of Dublin, 1417, New College, Oxford

The crozier, or cross, is usually held in the left hand. The mitred abbots wore exactly similar robes.

Bishop Wyvil of Salisbury, in three-quarter length, 1375, is shown within a battlemented castle with his champion standing under the gate beneath. This commemorates his recovery of Sherborne Castle for his See.

The Edenham brass (c. 1500) was formerly in a panel on the outer face of the church tower, 40 feet from the ground. It is now inside the church. Probably it represents St Thomas à Becket, the patron saint of the donor of the tower.

Bishop Goodryke of Ely, 1554, wrote "My duty towards my neighbour," and holds the prayer book in his hand. He also holds the Great Seal, as he was formerly Lord Chancellor. Both he and Bishop Bell died during the reign of Mary, which might be considered sufficient explanation of their wearing vestments. Bishop Pursglove, however, whose brass is at Tideswell, died in the middle of Elizabeth's reign.

The fact is that vestments only gradually fell into disuse. They were undoubtedly worn by some of the clergy right into the seventeenth century.

The figure of John Bell at St James's, Clerkenwell, the lower part of which is lost, was sold in 1788 when the old church was pulled down. It passed into the collection of Mr J. B. Nichols and on his death was replaced in the new church.

The vestments in which the king is crowned are largely of an ecclesiastical nature. They include the dalmatic, the surcoat, the belt, the stole and a surplice without sleeves. On monuments, kings are shown wearing a long tunic with close sleeves, a cloak, or cope, and a tippet of ermine. The only *brass* is a demi-figure, c. 1440, at Wimborne Minster, Dorset, laid down in memory of King Ethelred, martyred 872 A.D. He is crowned and holds a sceptre.

CHAPTER VI

THE MONASTERIES

THE influence of the monasteries during the Middle Ages was considerable, and it was in them that the lamp of learning and art was kept burning. The causes which led to their destruction would be too long a matter to discuss here. In justice we must say that the charges of gross immorality levied against the monks were neither fair nor were they the real reason for the dissolution of the monasteries.

The last monastery had fallen by 1540. In most cases the churches were destroyed, and even when they were preserved the brasses were taken from the gravestones and sold by the Commissioners who confiscated the property.

Thus at St Albans there were over 270 brasses, and now there are hardly a dozen. In all England there are barely 30 monastic brasses left. They include seven monks and a friar, two abbesses, a prior and five vowesses, besides one or two doubtful examples.

Besides the three abbots already mentioned as showing episcopal vestments, there are four mutilated fragments on the reverse of palimpsests (see below). These will be given in the list of palimpsests.

The dress of a monk included the tunic, an undergarment, with the gown over it, the scapula and cowl or hood. The tonsure is much larger than that of a parish priest.

Abbot John Lawrence at Burwell, 1542, was originally shown in full vestments, but as he survived the dissolution his brass was changed. He now appears in cassock, surplice and almuce. The upper part of the figure is new, but the lower shows on the reverse the original engraving. There is a canopy, part of which is palimpsest and shows, on the reverse, part of a deacon, c. 1320.

The Benedictines were by far the richest and largest of the Orders. The Cluniacs were a reformed order of Benedictines. The chief difference

VI] THE MONASTERIES 45

Fig. 16. Thomas Neolond, Prior of Lewes, 1433, Cowfold, Sussex

was that each monastery was under the direct supervision of Cluny, and not of the mother monastery from which it sprung. In England there was an exception and Lewes stood in the position of Cluny to the other English Cluniac monasteries. It alone was directly under Cluny.

Prior Neolond, here illustrated, was therefore a very important man. His dress is exactly similar to that of the Benedictines. The canopy, as shown, is the finest still extant of purely English type. The central pediment is itself triple and holds a shrine with the Virgin and Child within. St Pancras and St Thomas à Becket stand on the finials of the other pediments. The whole brass measures 10 ft. 2 in. × 4 ft. 3 in.

The Augustinian abbot wears gown and cowl over the ordinary choir vestments. The crozier rests on the right arm and he wears no mitre.

A vowess was a widow who took monastic vows. It is not easy to distinguish the dress from that of the ordinary widow.

The Duchess of Gloucester, after the murder of her husband in 1397, entered the nunnery at Barking, Essex, and died there two years later. She appears in the first act of *Richard II*. Her brass lies on an altar tomb in St Edmund's Chapel, Westminster Abbey. Her heraldic badge—the swan—adorns the inscription and the central pediment of her triple

VI] THE MONASTERIES 47

Fig. 17. Eleanor de Bohun, Duchess of Gloucester (Vowess), 1399. Westminster Abbey

canopy. Five armorial shields still hang from the shafts, but the sixth is lost. The pinnacle between the central and the sinister arch is now lost, but was still intact when this rubbing was taken. (See illustration.) Thus year by year portions of these ancient monuments are carelessly lost or stolen.

The friar, in gown and cowl, with knotted cord (c. 1440), at Denham, Bucks., is on the reverse of Amphillis Peckham, 1545.

The other brasses call for no further attention, save that in the case of the two nuns from Sion their convent had already been dissolved. The abbess is shown without her crosier and Margaret Dely without her mantle.

Palimpsest Brasses.

By this we mean brasses which have been twice used. The dissolution of the monasteries led to thousands of brasses being sold for old metal, both from the churches destroyed and from those that were allowed to remain. In 1551 an order was issued confiscating all the church plate. It is therefore not surprising that great numbers of brasses were stolen. It is noteworthy that Elizabeth disapproved of these proceedings and ordered that fresh plate should be procured, and that the damaged monuments should be restored. The stolen brasses often went into the melting pot, but sometimes they were re-engraved and used to commemorate contemporary persons.

THE MONASTERIES

Palimpsests are produced in three ways:

I. By engraving the back of the brasses.

II. By re-engraving and altering the figures.

III. By simply substituting a fresh inscription.

Those contained in the first group are probably the most numerous, and are subdivided into three groups:

(*a*) Plunder from English churches at the Reformation; (*b*) plunder from Flemish churches at the same period; (*c*) shop-wastes and earlier stolen brasses.

The Flemish or German brasses, about 50 in number, were probably plunder from the Dutch churches, which were sacked by the Calvinists in 1566. So complete was the destruction wrought in that short week that to-day there are fewer complete Flemish brasses in their original home than there are fragments of Flemish brasses in England. (See Appendix.)

The reverses vary considerably in date and subject. Those laid down from 1540–1570 show that even before the great outbreak of iconoclasm of 1566 a good many brasses had been stolen.

Taillor at Hadleigh, in Suffolk, was burnt during the Marian persecution in 1555, and an inscription was laid down in 1560. The reverse, c. 1500, shows the head and shoulders and hands of a civilian on a diapered background with certain other details. The Margate brass, 1582, shows on the reverse scenes from the life of man. One is of a child catching butterflies, and the other, two boys walking on stilts.

Besides these groups there is a third type consisting mostly of shop-wastes, i.e. sometimes a brass which had been ordered was not approved; the engraver then either melted it down or re-engraved it on the other side. Also, brasses were stolen and sold to the brass engravers, who would use them again in the same way. Many of these are quite early and often only a few years separate the engravings on the two sides.

In a few cases the same person is depicted with certain details altered. John Lawrence of Burwell has already been mentioned.

The demi-figure of Thos. Cod, St Margaret's, Rochester, 1465, is a striking example. The reverse shows him in almuce and cope, but for some unknown reason this apparently was disapproved. He is therefore shown on the obverse with an amice in place of the almuce.

A late example is at Walton-on-Thames. John Selwyn, 1587, was Gentleman Keeper of the Royal Park at Oatlands. At a stag-hunt in the presence of Elizabeth he leapt from his horse on to the back of the stag when both were going at full speed. There

THE MONASTERIES

he kept his seat, with his sword guided the animal towards the Queen, and then plunged the steel into its throat so that it fell dead at her feet.

This is depicted on a small plate placed between the heads of Selwyn and his wife. The subject is engraved on both sides. The reverse was lightly sketched and was rejected. It shows him hatless holding the stag's right horn.

The two remaining groups, II and III, are much less numerous. Group II consists of figures which have been altered.

Examples of this kind are Robt. Hanson, 1545, Chalfont St Peters, Bucks., altered (by adding shading, etc.) from a priest, 1440. Humphrey Oker and wife, 1538, Okeover, Staffs., altered from Wm. Lord Zouche and two wives, c. 1447. The figure of one wife was left intact and the other was turned over and engraved with the children and an oak-tree bearing a shield.

There are a few other examples, but perhaps the most interesting is that to Walter Curzon and wife, Waterperry, Oxon., 1527, altered from c. 1445. A new head and shoulders were engraved, the palettes were partly erased and shading was added on arms, cuirass and legs. The taces have been re-engraved to form a skirt of mail. The ends of the shoes have been partly erased and the toes rounded. The upper half of the lady is Tudor, the lower half has had shading added to the lines, and a chain hanging from the belt added.

Group III consists of appropriate brasses which have not been re-engraved. A new inscription, and sometimes shields, are merely added.

Good examples of this group are the brasses of Sir John Dyve, 1535, wife and mother, Bromham, Beds., appropriated from Thos. Wideville and two wives under triple canopy, c. 1435; John Wybarne (in armour), c. 1546, Ticehurst, Sussex, appropriated from c. 1370; Laughton, Lincs., 1549, man under triple canopy, appropriated from c. 1400; Joan ffenner, 1516, Horley, Surrey, appropriated from c. 1420, with fine canopy.

There are several other examples and they must be carefully distinguished from those brasses which have been *copied* from an earlier brass, as has happened in the effigy of Peter Rede at St Peter Mancroft, Norwich.

CHAPTER VII

THE EARLY TUDORS. 1485–1547

During this period more brasses were laid down than in the whole of the preceding time. Over 1100 belong to the reigns of Henrys VII and VIII. From Edward I to Richard III, 1000 were laid down.

VII] THE EARLY TUDORS, 1485-1547 53

But the work shows lamentable signs of steady deterioration; metal and engraving are usually poor, the former thin and the latter shallow and with too much detail. There is a greater variety of design, but many are in bad taste, such as figures shown in shrouds or as skeletons. At this date brasses are often placed on the wall, and sometimes are quadrangular. The latter must be carefully distinguished from foreign ones (see later).

Canopies are few and heavy, but continue to follow the traditional lines.

In the military brasses a sudden change becomes noticeable. The Yorkist armour is changed to the Tudor between 1490 and 1500. Its characteristics are that the placates are omitted, the pauldrons are single and have passe-gards to protect the neck, shorter tuilles are attached to the taces, a skirt of mail has been re-introduced and reaches well down over the thighs. The graceful, pointed sollerets—which must have been rather uncomfortable—were replaced by sabbatons with large rounded or square toes.

The sword is usually hung across the back of the legs. The hair is long and straight. Most of these and other characteristics will be seen in the illustration of John Shelley and wife, Clapham, Sussex, 1526. The Tabard of Arms covers the body armour.

The Yorkist armour was certainly more beautiful,

Fig. 18. John Shelley and wife, 1526, Clapham, Sussex

but one is apt to get rather an unfair impression from the brasses. There still survives a considerable amount of actual armour of this period, and from it we can see that it was often truly magnificent. At times it was engraved and embossed, and there are several variations not shown in the brasses, such as the skirt of plate. Those interested in the subject should study the fine collections at the Tower of London and elsewhere. It is most fortunate that our national collection of armour was begun just when the brasses by deterioration began to furnish less trustworthy evidence. Of the armour previous to the Yorkist period, practically none survives, hence the importance of the good engraving of the earlier brasses. (See Appendix.)

Serjeants-at-arms usually carry maces.

One of the most characteristic features of the period is the armorial tabard. Often, too, the wife has an armorial mantle: as in the brass of John Shelley and his wife, 1526, Clapham, Sussex, here shown. The arms are repeated on Shelley's sleeves and his wife bears her own arms impaling those of her husband on her mantle. The Holy Trinity is shown above the figures.

The tabard replaced the heraldic jupon of the Plantagenets during the Lancastrian period. The earliest is to John Wantele, 1424, Amberley, Sussex, but the arms are not repeated on the sleeves. There are but few examples, however, till the Yorkist period, and they only became plentiful under the Tudors. They died out in the opening years of Elizabeth, the last being to Sir John Tregonwell, Milton Abbey, Dorset, 1565.

Examples of Tabards of Arms during the Yorkist period are: Sir John Say and wife, Broxbourne, Herts., 1473, and Philip Mede and two wives, St Mary, Redcliff.

Lady Tiptoft at Enfield, Middlesex, c. 1470 (here illustrated), is a very splendid brass, and shows the armorial bearings well. (See Appendix.)

The colour of the coats-of-arms was probably shown by means of lead for *argent*, coloured earths for *colour*, and the plain brass for *or*. At Ardingley, Sussex, are three brasses in all of which the coloured earth is still in place. Unless this has been replaced later, it is a striking example, for in most cases all trace of the coloured earths has vanished. At Broxbourne, real enamel was used (as also at Stoke d'Abernon, 1279), and in consequence most of the colour is still in place.

It is held by some that all engraved lines on all brasses were filled in with black wax or some similar substance, just as in our modern inscriptions. That this was so in some cases seems certain, and at the Victoria and Albert Museum in the foreign brass to Henry Oskens (canon) from Nippes, near Cologne,

VII] THE EARLY TUDORS, 1485–1547 57

Fig. 19.
Lady Tiptoft (Partly covered),
c. 1470, Enfield, Middlesex

1535, much of the wax is still there. It is, of course, impossible to make a good rubbing of such a brass.

It does not seem likely that most of the brasses were so treated, but it would take too long to go into all the evidence which leads one to hold this view, nor is it desirable to use it now.

The ladies' dress also changes at the same time as their husbands'. The butterfly head-dress gives way to the kennel head-dress. This has a stiff point in front and is carried back like the roof of a kennel (hence the name) and has long side lappets, usually of embroidery. In some of the earlier examples these are pinned up (Ardingley), but, as a rule, they fall straight down (Clapham).

The dress is close-fitting and has a square collar and fur cuffs. Round the waist is a girdle with a chain pendant in front, to which is attached an ornament of varying shape. Occasionally mantles are worn, as at Cobham, Kent, but seldom, except when they bear a coat-of-arms.

Quite often babies will be found wrapped in chrysoms with swaddling bands round them. This robe was placed on the child by the priest as soon as it was baptised (which was when it was only a few days old). It was worn till the mother came to be churched, when it was returned to the priest. These brasses therefore show that the child died during the time that elapsed between baptism and the churching.

VII] THE EARLY TUDORS, 1485–1547 59

Chrysom children are found alone or with parents. This type of brass survived till the middle of the seventeenth century.

Occasionally brasses are found commemorating women who died in childbirth. The infant is then usually shown in a chrysom robe, and in later brasses the mother is often shown lying on a four-post bedstead. Anne Asteley, Blickling, Norfolk, 1512, probably belongs to this group. During the reign of Elizabeth, several examples of bedstead brasses are found. The first is at Heston, Middlesex, 1581, another is at Halling, Kent, 1587, and there are several others.

Fig. 20. Richard Wakehurst and wife, engr. c. 1500, Ardingley, Sussex

The civilians at this period are numerous, but not particularly interesting. The hair is long and straight, the gown reaches to the feet and is usually lined and edged with fur. The sleeves are wide, and a girdle surrounds the waist, from which hangs a short rosary and a purse. Broad-toed shoes are worn. The brass at Ardingley shows this dress, the canopy is an unusual feature.

CHAPTER VIII

EDWARD VI AND MARY. TRANSITIONAL PERIOD

DURING this period not more than sixty brasses were laid down. This was largely due to the religious and political turmoil of the period and is the more to be regretted, especially in the case of the clergy, as the brasses might have thrown much light on the question of the vestments worn during the time when the first and second Prayer Books of Edward VI were in use.

The engraving grows steadily poorer and the metal thinner.

Of the ecclesiastics, the following is believed to be a complete list for both reigns, but the Marian clergy, being naturally in full vestments, have for the most part been mentioned before.

Hugh Brystowe (parson), Waddesdon, Bucks. (in shroud), 1548.

VIII] EDWARD VI AND MARY 61

Jn. White (Warden of Winchester College and later Bp. of Winchester), Winchester College is in cope, laid down in 1548.
Thos. Magnus (archdeacon), Sessay, Yorks. (cope), 1550.
Bp. Goodryke of Ely, Ely Cathedral (full vestments), 1554.
Bp. Bell of Worcester, St James, Clerkenwell (ditto), 1556.
James Coorthorp (Dean of Peterborough), Christ Church, Oxford (in almuce), 1557.
Arthur Cole (Canon of Windsor), Magdalen College, Oxford (in mantle of the Order), 1558.
Robt. Brassie (in almuce), King's College, Cambridge, 1558.

The largest number of transitional brasses represent men in armour either with or without the tabard of arms.

The chief changes are that the mail skirt has often an indented edge, the taces are divided at the lower part by an arched opening between the tuilles, and frills are worn at the wrists.

The most noteworthy change in the ladies' attire is that the kennel head-dress is abandoned. The hair is parted in front and a linen cap supports a bonnet, often of velvet and having a jewelled edge. It is generally of horseshoe shape. A kerchief hangs down over the neck and shoulders behind. This head-dress is continued during the reign of Elizabeth and was known as the Queen Mary cap, at first after Mary Tudor, and later after Mary Stuart. The sleeves are slashed and puffed at the shoulders and from the belt hangs a mirror or other ornament. The collar is

thrown open and reveals a gathered underbodice.
A long cloak with false sleeves is often found, and
heraldic mantles are still worn when the husband
appears in a tabard. These died out in the opening
years of Elizabeth, as already stated.

Of civilians little need be said. Their wives follow
the new style, but little alteration in their own dress
is noticeable. Three examples may be given, the
last a woolman, the other two judges. These are
Henry Bradschawe and wife, Halton, Bucks., 1553;
Wm. Coke and wife, Milton, Cambridge, 1553;
Anthony Cave and wife, Chicheley, Bucks., 1558.

CHAPTER IX

ELIZABETH AND JAMES I. 1558–1625

DURING this last period there was a considerable
revival both in the number and quality of brasses.
About 800 were laid down in these two reigns and at
first there is a marked improvement in the engraving.
It is usual to speak as if the deterioration continued
steadily from the time of Henry VIII through the
Edwardian and Elizabethan brasses to the final
disappearance of the art in the eighteenth century.
This is not quite the case. The Elizabethan brasses
(with which are included those of James I) are

ix] ELIZABETH AND JAMES I 63

decidedly better in many instances than those of the Transitional period. Even some of the Caroline examples are better than those laid down between 1547 and 1558.

Early in the reign of Elizabeth, the plate of brass itself began to be manufactured in England. It was usually thin, however, and the engraving as in the Transitional brasses was shallow and too much detail and shading were attempted. The thinness of metal led to their becoming battered and worn and they are often in far worse condition than those laid down a couple of centuries earlier.

Many brasses were, however, fixed to the walls and these are in a much better state of preservation. These sometimes take the form of rectangular plates: at times the figures are fixed against the wall in a recess over a tomb. They are then usually depicted kneeling at desks.

The new style of armour which took the place of that worn in the Transitional period became finally established by 1575. Its main characteristics are these: The use of the long-waisted doublet and the short hose rendered the old style of armour unwearable. The cuirass becomes long and is brought forward to a peak with a projecting rim. It is known as a "peascod." The pauldrons are large and have no ridges, they are lined with leather the escalloped edge of which is allowed to extend beyond the plates. The neck is encircled by a ruff, as are the wrists. The helmet is seldom worn, but is often placed behind the head, though the figure is depicted standing.

Kneeling figures in many cases have the helmet on the ground, together with the gauntlets.

The front of the thighs are protected by laminated cuissarts under the trunk hose, and the legs by kneecaps and greaves. The sollerets are of a more graceful shape and fit the feet closely. Two long tassets are buckled to the edge of the cuirass, and hang down over the trunk hose. They are all formed of several hinged plates and take the place of tuilles. They are not infrequently rounded at the lower edge and are fastened by straps to the breeches. The sword hangs at the left side from a leather belt and the dagger at the right side from a sash. Swords usually possess guarded hilts.

The illustration of Wingfield, Easton, Suffolk, shows these characteristics, and there are but few variations. The most noticeable is where, the puffed breeches not being worn, continuous plates from knee to cuirass protect the legs. This type is shown in the brasses of Thos. Hawkins, Boughton-under-Blean, Kent, 1587, and Thos. Nevynson and wife, Eastry, Kent, 1590.

It is remarkable how, in spite of gunpowder being in general use, the men of the age of Elizabeth were still encased in a panoply of plate.

The ladies fall naturally into two divisions. The

ELIZABETH AND JAMES I

Fig. 21. John Wingfield, 1584, Easton, Suffolk

Transitional form, or Queen Mary dress, changed about 1560. The gown is fastened only at the waist by a sash, and thus shows below an embroidered or quilted petticoat. Between the bodice and the throat, the bust is covered by a gathered partlet with a frill and the Paris bonnet continues in use. From about 1575 a new style comes into vogue and is well shown in the illustration of the wife of Wm. Wade, Bildeston, Suffolk, 1599. Her skirt is distended at the hips by the farthingale and shows the embroidered petticoat beneath. The sleeves are slashed and a large ruff is round the neck. Usually frills are also worn at the wrists, but here Alice Wade is an exception. A broad-brimmed hat is worn.

There are several variations. The lappet of the bonnet is sometimes turned up over the head, and when it comes far enough forward to shade the face, it is called a "Shadow." At the end of the period, a large veil was substituted. Sometimes the hair is brushed up to a lace crown, supported by a wire frame. This fashion is shown in the brass of Margt. Chute, Marden, Hereford, 1614. She wears besides the wheel farthingale, a peaked stomacher, and a starched collar ornamented with point lace.

The bedstead brasses have already been mentioned in reference to the chrysom children, but are really a peculiarity of this period.

The civilian costume is not over-interesting, be-

IX] ELIZABETH AND JAMES I 67

HERE LYETH BVRIED WILLIAM WADE OF THIS PISHE, AND
ONE OF THE HEIGH COVNSTABLES OF THIS HVNDRED,
WHO HAD TO WIFE ALICE BOGGIS, BY WHOME HE HAD SIXE
CHILDREN LIVEINGE AT HIS DECEASE, TWOE SONNES VIZ.
WILLIAM & ROBTE, & FOWER DAVGHTERS VIZ ALICE ANN
IOANE & MARY, AND DIED THE XIX DAY OF FEBRVARY, 1599

Fig. 22. Alice, wife of William Wade, 1599, Bildeston, Suffolk

cause doublet and hose are usually covered by a long gown, such as is seen in the memorial to Wm. Dunche and wife, quadrilateral plate, Little Wittenham, Berks., engraved c. 1585. Here husband and wife kneel at desks under two classical arches. Two sons kneel behind their father. They wear short cloaks, doublet and hose. This is also the costume of the sons of Alice Wade, who wear pointed beards.

The brasses of children, especially boys, become fairly numerous and are not without interest, as they exhibit the doublet and hose under a short cloak. The brass of W. Browne, Holton, Oxon., 1599, is a good example, showing the long hose fastened above the knee by garters of ribbon.

The clergy for the most part wear the ordinary civilian dress of the day without cassock or surplice, and a long gown with long sleeves, known as the Geneva gown. Some also wear a hood to denote they hold a degree, as does Dr Wm. Bill, Dean of Westminster, Westminster Abbey, 1561.

Of clergy in surplice and cassock only two brasses now survive. Formerly at Denham, Bucks., there was one portraying Leonard Hurst, 1561, in cassock and surplice opening in front like a college surplice and a long scarf. It is now lost, but is illustrated in Haine's *Manual*. The two that still survive are Wm. Dye (priest), Westerham, Kent, 1567, who wears cassock, a closed and gathered surplice and a scarf, and

IX] ELIZABETH AND JAMES I

Nich. Asheton, Winchford, Warwick, 1582, very similar to the lost brass at Denham, Bucks.

The remaining clergy are in civilian costume, but one or two wear a scarf over the Geneva gown, as at Stonham Aspall, 1606.

In many cases the title of the ecclesiastic is given, and these are of some interest. (See Appendix.)

Tyndall's figure is 5 ft. 4 in. long and there is a border fillet and several shields.

There are three bishops, but Robt. Pursglove, 1579, is in full mass vestments, and has been mentioned before.

Edmund Geste, Bishop of Salisbury, in his Cathedral, 1578, wears rochet and chimere, a scarf and lawn sleeves. Instead of a crozier, he holds a walking stick in his right and a book in his left hand. It should be remembered that this was the outdoor garb, hence probably the walking stick.

H. Robinson, Bishop of Carlisle, 1616, has two brasses, that at Queen's College, Oxford, being copied and put over his grave in Carlisle Cathedral. His brass, like Airay's, who succeeded him as Provost of Queen's, differs from the usual type. They resemble the copper plates used in books and are very finely engraved and filled with many additional emblems. A good rubbing cannot be taken owing to the thinness of the engraving, which nevertheless is well done.

On a quadrilateral plate, Robinson kneels in front

of Queen's College and Carlisle Cathedral. There are three sheep folds to signify he was a shepherd to his flock. Several peasants with their tools and in the dress of the period stand in one corner and dons are entering Queen's College in the other. He wears a skull cap and ruff, rochet and chimere. In his left hand he holds his crozier, which has a human eye in the centre, and a stork on the outer curve of the volute. The infula is a napkin and bears the word "Velando."

From the Elizabethan period some attempt at portraiture is made: in the case of Robinson and Airay with considerable success. The brass to Erasmus Williams, Rector at Tingewick, Bucks., 1608, is probably by the same hand as these two and is signed R. Haydock. It is very similar in general treatment to them, and on Airay's brass are the same initials R. H.

CHAPTER X

THE CAROLINE BRASSES. 1625–60

The art of monumental brasses shows signs of rapid deterioration, and from it there was to be no recovery. About 150 were laid down during the reign of Charles I and 13 during the Commonwealth.

Only two are really fine: Archbp. Harsnett's

Fig. 23. Sir Edward Filmer and family, 1638, East Sutton, Kent

brass at Chigwell, 1631, and Sir Edw. Filmer's, here shown.

Armour is seldom worn, knights being usually depicted in civilian dress, and where it is worn, it generally consists of a demi-suit of cuirass, with laminated plates for the thighs and small knee pieces. Jack boots protect the legs. There are many variations, but the brass of Sir Edw. Filmer and wife, East Sutton, Kent, is fairly typical.

Of the nine sons, only one wears armour and none wear ruffs. The eight daughters are similar to their mother, who wears a gown without farthingale and a veil over the head. The brass consists of two large rectangular plates and though too much shading is put in, yet is a good example for the period.

The ladies have abandoned the farthingale and wear more graceful gowns, sometimes with ruffs and sometimes with falling collars. A light veil often covers the head. Sometimes the embroidered petticoat can be seen underneath the gown, which is divided in front. An example is to be found at Ardingley, Sussex, to Eliz. Culpeper, aged 7, 1634, and also in a larger brass to her mother.

The civilians are still fairly numerous, but the engraving is usually poor. The long gown is worn no more, the costume being the tunic with falling collar, knee-breeches, stockings and shoes or jack boots and a short cloak. Sometimes a ruff is worn instead of a

THE CAROLINE BRASSES, 1625–60

collar. Most of these details will be seen in the sons of Sir Edw. Filmer. Point lace was often worn and is occasionally seen, as in the small, badly engraved brass of Thos. Holl, 1630.

The brass of John Moorwood and wife is characteristic. He kneels opposite his wife, Grace, at a desk. Besides the costume described above, he wears a ruff and a skull cap. His hair is long and he has a moustache and a pointed beard. His sons are similar, save that they are hatless and have no beard or moustache. His wife has a very plain dress and a high-crowned hat, her daughters have no ruffs, veils, or bonnets.

The six at Llanrwst, Denbigh, are quite distinct and represent either the work of a local school or of a special artist. There was also a local school at York. Its peculiarity was that the figures were large demi-figures, usually on a quadrilateral plate, which was narrower at the top than at the bottom. A considerable amount of fur is displayed, and the faces appear to be good portraits. The Elizabethan have already been mentioned in the last chapter, but there are several others.

There is one good Caroline brass—that to Thos. Atkinson, All Saints, North St., York, 1642. It may have been engraved a few years earlier.

Among ecclesiastics there is but one fine example, and that is perhaps the best Caroline brass still extant. It commemorates Samuel Harsnett, Archbp. of York at Chigwell, Essex, 1631. He had left special instructions in his will as to how it was to be made. The metal was to be an inch thick and to be rivetted right through the stone so that it could not easily be torn up. The result is a fine monument. He wears cope, rochet, chimere and a mitre. He holds his crozier in his left hand and a book in the right. The face is evidently a portrait. There is a border inscription with the evangelists at the corners. The figure is 6 ft. long. The crozier is not a cross, but a crook and has a rose in the volute.

During the Commonwealth naturally few brasses were laid down, and the distrust with which all representations of the human form were regarded by the Puritans, who considered them a breach of the Second Commandment, probably gave the death blow to the failing art. Besides those already mentioned, the following have been noticed: Ralph Assheton (in armour) and wife, Middleton, Lancs., 1650; Adam Beaumont (in armour) and wife, Kirkheaton, Yorks., 1655. These are the only men in armour. Assheton was a leader on the Puritan side and did good service. Beaumont was his son-in-law and is clad in similar style. The armour is a demi-suit, consisting of skirted cuirass, pauldrons, elbow-pieces and laminar cuissarts extending to the top of his tall boots.

THE CAROLINE BRASSES, 1625–60

There is no actual representations of a cleric, but Dan. Evance, rector, quadrilateral plate, Calbourne, I.o.W., 1652 is commemorated by a plate with a drawing of Time and Death.

Most of these are but miserable caricatures and reveal the final stage of decay. Yet they are not without interest, though perhaps a melancholy one.

During the Caroline period many brasses to young children were laid down. Sometimes the babe is shown lying on a tomb, at others it is represented in its cradle. Two in St George's Chapel, Windsor, may be quoted, and commemorate the children of Dr John King. They are dated 1630 and 1633.

CHAPTER XI
THE LAST BRASSES. 1660–1773

THE last few brasses are of little artistic value. (See Appendix.)

Robt. Shiers, 1668, is perhaps the best of them. He wears a long, flowing gown reaching to the feet and holds a book in his hand. Nicholas Toke is in Jacobean armour, but with a fall collar and long hair. Probably his figure was copied from an earlier brass, for his daughters, who are on a separate plate, are very crudely drawn.

The last two brasses are the only Georgian ones known to exist and they are separated by a great space of time from the others. Whether they were each engraved at the dates given on the plates or whether they were both done at the same time is difficult to say. Benjamin Greenwood's brass is certainly the best, his wife's figure being very crude. She has on a plain gown and a veil. He is in a coat with open skirts, a figured waistcoat, knee-breeches, and wig. He points to a skull with his left hand and to a ship with his right. Probably he was a merchant captain.

Both plates have a pair of cherubs' heads in the upper corners and are upon separate gravestones; the engraving is very thin.

Thus we have seen the art of the engravers rise in the thirteenth century and die in the eighteenth.

CHAPTER XII

SPECIAL TYPES

BESIDES the ordinary figure brasses, there are a certain number of special types. Those representing Scriptural subjects are perhaps the most interesting. They are less numerous than might be expected and usually form part of a canopy, or, at any rate, part of a composition which includes large figures.

The Holy Trinity is the most common emblem and is depicted as a venerable man seated, holding

Christ crucified. The Holy Ghost in the form of a dove is sometimes perched on one arm of the Cross, or hovers over the head, but it is often omitted.

The Holy Trinity is found at Cobham, 1407; Peperharrow, 1487; Shirburn, 1493, and Witney, Oxon., 1500; Childrey, Berks., 1507; Floore, Northants., 1510; Wooburn, Bucks., 1520; Clapham, Sussex, 1526; Beaumaris, Anglesea, c. 1530; Cheam, Surrey, 1542.

The Virgin is found at Cobham, 1395; Bottesford, Leics., 1404; Morley, Derbys., 1470; Etwall, Derbys., 1512; St George's Chapel, Windsor, 1522; and elsewhere.

Numerous other saints are depicted as well as those in canopy niches and on the orphreys of copes.

The Annunciation is found in several places. That at Fovant, Wilts., 1492, is contained in a rectangular plate commemorating Geo. Rede, rector. He wears cassock and scarf, kneels on a chequered pavement and prays to the Virgin, who, dressed in mantle, sideless *cote-hardi* and kirtle, with a wreath of roses on her head, kneels at a *prie-dieu* in the centre of the plate. A pot of lilies stands behind her and an angel kneels on the further side, wearing an alb and mantle. The Dove flies towards the Virgin from a cloud in the corner. The whole composition is reminiscent of foreign work, but is almost certainly English. An Annunciation is to be seen at March, Cambs. (1517), above the figures of Antony Hansart and his wife. A third is in the canopy of William Porter, S.T.P., 1524, Hereford Cathedral.

The Adoration of the Shepherds is found at Cobham, Surrey, c. 1500.

The Resurrection is more widely distributed, and in two forms according as (*a*) there are or (*b*) are not soldiers round the tomb.

Of class (*a*), those at Swansea, c. 1500; Cranley, Surrey, 1503; All Hallows, Barking, c. 1510; and Narburgh, Norfolk, 1545, are characteristic.

Of class (*b*), examples may be seen at Stoke Charity, Hants., 1482; Stoke Lyne, Oxon., 1535 and Burwell, Cambs., 1542. Of this latter class, the Burwell brass is the best. The Saviour's form is unclothed and the lower half hidden within the tomb; His hands are raised and He holds no cross.

Class (*a*) is the more interesting. The Cranley and Swansea representations are the best. In the former, which is to Robt. Hardyng and his wife, 1503, Christ steps from the sarcophagus unclothed save for a loin cloth. Four out of the five wounds are thus plainly shown. He holds a cross (in His left hand) bearing a pennon, with a cross in its centre. A nimbus is around His head. The four soldiers are clad in armour with morions on their heads and halberts in their hands.

XII] SPECIAL TYPES 79

The Swansea representation measures 12 × 11 inches and is to Sir Hugh Johnys and his wife, c. 1500. He was a knight of the Holy Sepulchre, and fought against the Turks under John, at that time Emperor of Constantinople. One of the soldiers round the tomb evidently represents a Saracen. He is shown sleeping with a scimitar at his left, a spiked mace at his right side.

One other curious pictorial example must not be omitted. It represents the Mass of St Gregory. The Pope kneels before an altar, while the figure of our Lord rises from behind the chalice, changed from the consecrated wafer. It is in the brass of Roger Legh and wife (lost), Macclesfield, Cheshire, 1506, and is unique. The original story is in the *Golden Legend*.

Heart Brasses.

The next curious type is that known as Heart Brasses. A heart is often shown held in the hands of the deceased, as at Buslingthorpe, Lincs., c. 1290. At other times it is found quite separate from the figure and often with two or three inscribed scrolls coming from it. Thos. Knyghtley, Fawsley, Northants., 1516, is typical of this class.

But the name applies more especially to those monuments in which the heart appears alone. Often these doubtless marked the spot where the heart alone was buried. We have many authentic records of men who ordered their hearts to be buried apart from their bodies. Some of these were knights who perished abroad and ordered their bodies to be buried where they died, but their hearts to be brought back to England. From the inscription upon one of the four scrolls of the Wiggenhall brass, *Cuius cor hic humatur*, we may reasonably infer that the heart only lies beneath the stone. There are several stone monuments showing only hearts, which records prove cover only that organ. Thus, Sir Thos. Neville's body was buried at Birling, 1535, and his heart at Mereworth, Kent. At the latter place his stone monument consists of a heart held by two hands.

Heart brasses proper fall into two main divisions: (*a*) plain, sometimes inscribed or with scrolls, (*b*) held by hands, usually coming out of a cloud.

Class (*a*) includes Thos. Smyth, priest, St John's, Margate, Kent, 1433; an unknown person, Kirby Bedon, Norfolk, c. 1450; and Sir Robt. Kervile, Wiggenhall St. Mary, Norfolk, c. 1450.

Good representatives of class (*b*) are the brasses of John Merstun, priest, Lillingstone Lovell, Oxon., 1446; Wm. Stapilton, Helbroughton, Norfolk, c. 1450; Dionysius Willys, Loddon, Norfolk, 1462; and Thos. Denton, Caversfield, Bucks., 1533. (See Appendix.)

XII] SPECIAL TYPES 81

Shrouds.

These and the following group are neither beautiful nor pleasing monuments. They are signs of the morbid feeling that seems to have begun to spread over England about the middle of the fifteenth century and which did not pass away until the nineteenth.

Many stone monuments exist showing reclining figures in the costume of the period on a raised tomb, while beneath, visible through openings in the sides, are the same persons shown as skeletons or shrouded figures. This contrast is seldom exhibited in *brasses*, but the kneeling figure of Lionel Dymoke, Horncastle, Lincs. (1519), in armour, is engraved upon a small plate on the wall, while on the pavement below he is represented by a shrouded figure.

In some cases the brass was laid down on the death of one of those commemorated. The latter is then shown in a shroud, while those who survived are shown in the dress of the period.

Women can be recognised by their long, flowing hair, and priests by their tonsure. The purpose of this type of brass was probably to remind us that "such as we are, such shall ye be." (See Appendix.)

Under the Tudors, this type of brass increased in favour, and its persistence is remarkable.

The last brass of 1660 was probably inspired by the earlier one of 1505.

At Childrey, c. 1520, husband and wife rise from their tombs, but at Oddington devouring worms crawl out of the body, which is almost a skeleton.

This leads us to

Skeletons.

They are not so common as shroud brasses, but belong to the same class. Indeed, some of the former are really shrouded skeletons.

Other designs.

A few other designs may be found scattered up and down the country. Perhaps the most interesting is to Roger Morris, Margate, Kent, 1615. He was an official in the Navy and his brass consists of a square plate showing a three-masted square rigged man-o'-war. It has a lion figure-head, high poop and many guns showing through the port holes.

CHAPTER XIII

FOREIGN BRASSES

BRASSES on the Continent, as already stated, were engraved on quadrilateral plates, the inscription, canopy and background, all being engraved on the same plates, there is therefore no background of stone, as in England. Any space left over was usually filled with diaper work or some similar pattern. Many of those which still survive on the Continent are remarkably splendid. There were originally at least three great schools, besides several minor subdivisions. These were the German, Flemish, and French. The Revolutionaries destroyed almost all those in France and the Reformers played sad havoc with the Dutch and German monuments. Still, many fine examples remain of the German and Flemish schools. The former are found at Ringstead, Denmark, engr. c. 1350, to King Eric and Queen Ingeborg, at Lübeck, Schwerin, Stralsund (Pomerania), Thorn and elsewhere. The latter exist at Ghent 14th c., Brussels 1398, Bruges 15th c. Most of these were Hanse towns and all carried on trade with England. Merchants from them settled in England and in some cases had their brasses made abroad. It thus came about that 14 remain of undoubtedly foreign work, besides two which were bought abroad and are now in the Victoria and Albert Museum. These form an entirely separate group and must be dealt with apart.

On the other hand, one English brass is known to exist on the Continent. It is at Constance, to the memory of an English bishop who died at the Council of Constance.

The finest foreign brasses are those of the fourteenth century, and are as follows: Adam de Walsokne and wife, King's Lynn, Norfolk, 1349 ; Abbot Thos. Delamere, St Albans Abbey, c. 1360; Simon de Wenslagh, priest, Wensley, Yorks., c. 1360 ; a Priest, North Mimms, Herts., c. 1360 ; Robt. Braunche and two wives, King's Lynn, Norfolk, 1364 ; Ralph de Knevyngton (in armour, small) Aveley, Essex, 1370 ; Alan Fleming, Newark, Notts., c. 1375 ; and Thos. de Topclyffe and wife, Topcliffe, Yorks., 1391.

There seems little doubt that these fall into two schools—North German and Flemish.

The first may be called North German, and five brasses of Hanseatic merchants are so exactly alike that they must come from the very same workshop. They are the two at King's Lynn and one each at St Peter's, Lübeck, 1356, at Thorn, 1357, and at Stralsund, 1361.

The trefoils on the background are similar, and so are the cushions on which rest the heads of the figures. A woodhouse (a wild man) struggles with an animal between the feet of the merchant, in each case.

The most interesting feature in each is that beneath the feet of the figures a long compartment is reserved for a scene. In the Walsokne brass, a horseman carrying corn to be ground at a mill is followed by two men bearing their master on a litter. There are also hunting scenes and a forester fighting with an outlaw. In the Braunche brass there is a representation (probably) of the mayor's feast at Lynn. Braunche was mayor in 1349 or 1359. The three peacocks are being borne by fair ladies heralded by trumpets.

There is in every brass a magnificent canopy with figures either of saints or of " weepers" in niches. The soul, a small naked figure, is being borne aloft by angels to God the Father.

The large number of figures included may be judged when we consider that the Walsokne brass has 57 alone. The principal figures are clad in the civilian costume already described, and their wives in the mantle, sideless *cote-hardi* and kirtle. In some the mantle is omitted, when it is easier to see the beautiful figured pattern with which the kirtle is adorned.

The Walsokne brass measures 9 ft. 10 in. × 5 ft. 8 in., and the Braunche 8 ft. 10 in. × 5 ft. 1 in., and some of the Continental ones are even larger.

The second group springs from a second workshop and includes three ecclesiastical brasses and the Royal brass at Ringstead. The former are at St Albans,

Lübeck and Schwerin (1347) respectively. The distinguishing feature of this group is that the cushions are omitted. A few other details differ, but in the main they follow the same lines as the others of North Germany. These two sub-groups probably both came from Lübeck, but are by different hands.

The Newark brass is also North German, but of later work than the other, for, though dated 1361, it was probably engraved about 1375. The most striking difference is that the canopy is drawn in perspective, with very unsatisfactory results. It is rather similar to the huge brass of Bishops Godfrey and Frederic de Bulowe at Schwerin, 1375. The latter measures 13 ft. 6 in. × 6 ft. 5 in. and is the largest in the world. The Newark brass measures 9 ft. 4 in. × 5 ft. 7 in. It is unfortunately much worn, and has been removed from its original position and placed against the wall.

The Wensley brass is also North German. The robes of the priest are embroidered in a similar design to those of Abbot Delamere, but there is no canopy or background.

The North Mimms brass is similar, but not so well engraved and the figure is only 27 inches long. The canopy has niches with the apostles, two angels with censor and the soul in the arms of the Father. There is no background, but probably it was cut away by the English workmen who laid it in the stone to make

XIII] FOREIGN BRASSES 87

it suit English ideas. The composition rises from a bracket on which is a coat-of-arms and two lions.

The Aveley and Topcliffe brasses are almost certainly Flemish. The former is very small, but beautifully engraved; there is a canopy, and the background has no design, being simply cross-hatched. The other brass measures 5 ft. 9 in. × 3 ft. 1 in. and represents a civilian and his wife. The ground work is a diaper pattern, and there is a fine canopy. On the reverse of several pieces earlier work exists and in one place a Flemish inscription.

There are five other English brasses of foreign work, and two foreign ones are in the Victoria and Albert Museum. There are also a few fragments among the palimpsests (see Chap. VI) and a fragment in the British Museum. (See Appendix.)

CHAPTER XIV

ARCHITECTURAL DETAILS[1]

BRASSES frequently contain a considerable amount of architectural detail in their composition. Sometimes they were placed on altar tombs under stone canopies, but it is of those details depicted in the brass itself that the author purposes to write.

[1] See special articles on this subject by the author in *The Builder*, vol. CII.

Canopies are by far the most important group, and the magnificence of some of these can be but faintly realised from the illustrations.

The earliest follow the Decorated style which was in fashion when they were laid down.

The first type consists of slender shafts supporting a pediment, of which the upper sides are straight, forming a triangle ornamented with crockets and terminated by a bunch of foliage. The arch beneath is trefoil and the cusps are filled with leaves. This form lasted from 1300 to c. 1325, but unfortunately only one example survives—that of Joan de Cobham, Cobham, Kent, 1320 (cf. p. 7). The side shafts were missing, but have, we believe, been restored. This is the second lady to be depicted on a brass, and she leads the fine series of nineteen brasses at Cobham. The slab of Margarete de Camoys, Trotton, Sussex, c. 1310, shows the matrix of a similar canopy. The fragments of the canopy of Sir Hugh Hastings, 1347, Elsing, Norfolk, also appear to belong to this type, but with later variations. In it, as in the canopy of Lawrence de St Maur, the canopies in the shafts are straight-sided.

This low pedimental form was soon superseded by the ogee arch rising to a considerable height. This is supported by equally tall side shafts. Sometimes, in place of a bunch of foliage, figures of saints are seen on the finial, as on several examples at

XIV] ARCHITECTURAL DETAILS 89

Cobham, Kent, notably Lady Margaret (cf. p. 13). At other times a shield with a coat-of-arms takes its place, as in the brass of Archbishop Waldeby, Westminster Abbey, 1397.

The next development was to widen the shafts, so as to form panels or niches containing canopied saints. Often these are surmounted by a super-canopy. The brass of Lawrence de St Maur, Higham Ferrers, Northants. (cf. frontispiece) shows this type. Canopies over mass priests are very rare and this is by far the finest. The details have been given before, so we will turn to another variation of this type.

Instead of canopy and super-canopy, an embattled canopy with an ogee pediment within is found. A splendid example is to a former Dean of St Asaph's and rector of Balsham, John Blodwell, 1462 (cf. p. 37). It measures 8 ft. 9 in. × 4 ft. 1 in.

Another development was, in place of a single arch to have double or triple arches. The former type was used almost exclusively where two persons were commemorated. The latter was sometimes used over three figures, but more often over one. Thus in the brass of the Duchess of Gloucester, Westminster Abbey, 1399 (cf. p. 47), we have a truly magnificent brass. Five shields hang from the shafts (the sixth is lost) and between the finials of her triple canopy are two other finials, one of which has been lost since this rubbing was made. A tabernacle with the Holy Trinity is often placed above the ogee arch in place of the central finial, as in the brass of Sir Nicholas Hawberk, Cobham, Kent, 1407. But not only the finest of this group, but of all *English* brasses now extant is the monument to Thomas Neolond, Cluniac Prior of Lewes, at Cowfold, Sussex, 1433 (cf. p. 45). This has a tabernacle with the Virgin and Child, and, moreover, the finials of the other two arches support St Pancras and St Thomas à Becket. Further, the central arch is also triple, and the shafts are supported by side shafts and connected by flying buttresses, as is likewise the tabernacle. The entire scheme is very graceful and recalls the lantern at Ely in its lightness. It is 10 ft. 2 in. × 4 ft. 3 in. A somewhat similar brass is that to John Sleford at Balsham, 1401.

The earlier canopies were not groined, one of the earliest exceptions being that over Lord Nicholas Burnell, Acton Burnell, Salop, 1382 (cf. p. 11). But during the fifteenth century this became more common (see the canopy of John Bloxham and John Wytton). It is an unsatisfactory feature, and characteristic of the gradual deterioration and coarsening of the engraving. This latter is also shown by the heavy finials and crockets.

In the sixteenth century, these peculiarities became more marked, though canopies still follow the

XIV] ARCHITECTURAL DETAILS 91

traditional lines. There are two or three early Renaissance canopies, e.g. a large, triple one to Wm. Porter, S.T.P., Hereford Cathedral, 1524, and Dean Frowsetoure, in cope, Hereford Cathedral, 1529.

It is difficult to say whether the classical arches shown in a few of the later brasses can be termed canopies. An example is to be found to Wm. Dunche and wife, Little Wittenham, Berks. (double) engr., c. 1585. (See Appendix.)

Brackets.

The idea of this group probably originated with the brackets supporting figures of saints, which were common in our churches before the Reformation. The brackets usually projected from a wall or column, and a small pillar helped to support them. Above was a canopy of carved stone or wood.

One would naturally expect that, if this idea were copied, the bracket would hold a saint and the deceased would kneel before it. There are, however, only two examples extant. The brass of John Spycer and wife, Burford, Oxon., 1437, is terribly mutilated. The canopy and Virgin and Child are lost, and only the deceased couple remain, kneeling on either side of the stem. The other example is practically complete and is to John Strete (priest in academics), Upper Hardres, Kent, 1405 (cf. p. 93). St Peter and St Paul stand on the bracket, and there is no canopy.

In all other cases the deceased persons themselves stand on the bracket. The earlier ones are much mutilated, and only one fourteenth century brass is at all perfect. It is to Sir John Foxley and two wives, Bray, Berks., 1378. The canopy is lost. The three figures are on a bracket with a short stem rising from the back of a fox, the family crest. The total length of the composition is just over 5 ft. Though the ladies are standing, the knight rests with his head on his helm and his feet on a lion.

The fifteenth century brasses are far more complete. (See Appendix.)

The Merton College brass is one of the finest. The stem rises from a tabernacle holding the Lamb with the banner.

In the sixteenth century should be noted the brasses of Sir Roger le Strange, Hunstanton, Norfolk, 1506; John Terry and wife, St John, Maddermarket, Norwich, 1524; John Marsham and wife, St John, Maddermarket, Norwich, 1525; and Robt. Rugge and wife, St John, Maddermarket, Norwich, 1558.

Sir Roger stands on a low bracket without a stem, placed *within*, not supporting, a magnificent canopy with figures of weepers in the side shafts.

The other three evidently come from a local school of engravers. Terry's bracket resembles a tree, the

XIV] ARCHITECTURAL DETAILS 93

Fig. 24. John Strete, M.A. 1405, Upper Hardres, Kent

branches support pedestals for himself, his wife and for his children. The whole is on a single plate. The Marsham bracket has a stem like that of a table and the top is covered with skulls and bones. In the Rugge brass there is only a corbel supporting an inscription.

So far as is known, there are no later bracket brasses.

Crosses.

These also form a group which may conveniently be dealt with here. At one time they were very numerous, but provoked the wrath of the Reformers more than any other type of brass, hence barely thirty remain. Matrices are still numerous and many might doubtless be restored as has been successfully done at Ely.

They fall into three main divisions: (1) plain crosses, (2) crosses with some saint in the centre, (3) crosses with the deceased in the centre.

This last group may be sub-divided into: (*a*) quatrefoil, (*b*) octofoil. (See Appendix.)

(1) These vary considerably in form. At Higham Ferrers, the arms terminate in the Evangelistic symbols. At Royston, a bleeding heart and the four wounds are shown. At Eversley, the whole cross is formed of interlocking bands, or links of a

XIV] ARCHITECTURAL DETAILS 95

Fig. 25. Robert de Paris and wife, 1379, Hildersham, Cambs.

chain. The cross at Floore, Northants., is drawn in perspective.

(2) There are but few examples of the second type. The best is to Robt. de Paris and wife, Hildersham, Cambs., 1379, here shown. The figures kneel on either side of a cross with an octofoil head, in which is the Holy Trinity. Robt. de Paris wears a long cloak, thrown open so as to show his undergarment, which stops short above the knees. A belt holds an anlace and his legs are covered with long hose.

Another example is that of John Mulsho and wife, Newton-by-Geddington, Northants., c. 1400, commemorated by a quatrefoil cross, holding a figure of St Faith. This brass was restored by Messrs Waller, but there seems little reason to doubt that the design is correct.

The brass of Robt. de Brun (priest), Chelsfield, Kent, 1417, is a much mutilated crucifix; the figure of St John is lost, the head of the Virgin and most of the cross. On the ground are Adam's skull, Jacob's ladder and the jawbone of an ass. The latter refers to the scriptural legend that from it flowed a stream of water to revive Samson's spirit (Judges xv. 19).

(3) (*a*) This division includes a small group of much interest. Some of the earliest belong to it, and many others—of the fourteenth century—have

perished. They are used to commemorate priests. These are: Rich. de Hakebourne (priest), Merton College, Oxford, c. 1310; A Priest, Chinnor, Oxford, c. 1320; Nichol. de Gore (priest), Woodchurch, Kent, c. 1320; and Britell Avenel (priest), Buxted, Sussex, 1408.

The first three brasses have lost their stems. The Merton and Chinnor crosses hold a demi-figure and a head respectively. Nicholas de Gore is a small, full-length figure, and the composition is very pleasing. The Buxted cross is the only one which is nearly perfect. The priest is a demi-figure, resting on a diapered background. There is a border inscription.

(b) Octofoil crosses are more numerous. Those at East Wickham, 1325, and Wimbish, 1347, have already been described.

The East Wickham brass had the missing parts restored in 1887. The Taplow cross (c. 1350) rises from a dolphin, an appropriate emblem for a fishmonger.

The octofoil consists of eight ogee arches, alternately large and small, with finials of foliage.

Other Architectural Features.

There are several brasses in which architectural features are included which do not come under these headings. Thus, Bishop Wyvil, Salisbury Cathedral, 1375, is shown as a demi-figure within a castle, with his champion at the portcullis below. This commemorates his recovery of the Castle of Sherborne for the See. There are several rabbits at the foot of the castle, and these probably commemorate his recovery of a piece of ground known as "The Warren."

Bp. Robinson's brass shows Carlisle Cathedral and Queen's College, Oxford, and many sixteenth century brasses show walls, pillars, etc.

In an interesting series of three sixteenth century brasses, probably by the same hand, to Robt. Honywode, St George's Chapel, Windsor, 1522; Robt. Sutton, St Patrick's, Dublin, 1528; and Geoff. Fyche, St Patrick's, Dublin, 1537; what is really a view of a side-chapel is shown.

At Windsor, beneath the Tudor arch, Honywode kneels at a *prie-dieu* before a statue of the Virgin and Child. In the Irish examples, the resemblance to a side-chapel is still more complete. Fyche kneels at a faldstool before an altar with a picture above it of the descent from the Cross. The vaulting of part of the roof is visible, and the walls have linenfold panelling. A shield hangs from a hook at one side bearing a bush with several birds on it and the initials F. G., which evidently refer to and are probably meant as a pun on his name—Finch for Fyche.

XIV] ARCHITECTURAL DETAILS 99

The floor is laid with tiles and a Renaissance arch forms a kind of canopy in the foreground. Parts of rooms are often shown in sixteenth century brasses.

In a few cases, brasses were laid down to founders of churches. They usually hold a model of the church in their hands. An example exists at Cobham, to Sir John de Cobham, 1365. The building is in the decorated style, has a small spire and a large porch.

CHAPTER XV

CONCLUSION

THE great fascination of monumental brasses can only be realised by studying them on the spot. One of the best methods is to take rubbings of them.

Most of our readers doubtless know the method, but since a few may not, some particulars are appended.

A piece of cobbler's wax should be procured from some boot repairer. The black kind is the only one which produces satisfactory results on white paper. It can usually be got in small lumps about the size of a halfpenny across. Melt down six of these to make a single ball. Procure a roll of plain white

7—2

ceiling paper, the thinner the better, from a paper-hanger's. It should cost from 6*d.* to 8*d.* according to quality. A penny nail-brush and a duster complete the outfit.

First ask permission from the Rector or Vicar. This should not be omitted, and will avoid unpleasantness. The clergy are usually most considerate in the matter, and very rarely refuse. But naturally they do not like absolute strangers to take rubbings without first asking permission. So far as the writer knows, permission is refused only at *two* churches, though probably there are a few others. In those cases the reason given was that it wore away the brass. We have never seen any real cause to think this can be correct. If we did, we should be the last to advocate brass-rubbing.

There *is* a kind of rubbing which does damage. Well-meaning vergers have been known to *polish* an old brass. This is absolutely destructive of the engraving.

Permission granted, remove the mat which probably covers and protects it. Brush off the accumulated dust, finishing off with the duster. Then carefully spread the paper over it and fix it down by weights round the edge. For these, hassocks are handy; prayer-books should be avoided, their misuse causes offence.

Then rub the paper down well with a *clean* part

of the duster, so as to mark the main features and edges, and after that the rubbing with the wax ball itself will be easy.

The aim should be to produce a clear, dark impression. To get it, the rubbing must be hard and the paper must not slip. If there is a canopy, it will probably be found that the wax will mark parts of the paper beyond the design itself. In such a case, the rubbing should be cut out and mounted on paper or calico. Paste is better than gum for this purpose. The rubbing should always be polished by rubbing over with a clean part of the duster *before* being removed from the brass.

The completed rubbing may be mounted on rollers.

A good way of cataloguing, is to photograph each rubbing, mount a print in a book, and then number and name print and rubbing alike.

The proper treatment of the brasses themselves demands considerable attention. We spend huge sums on buying old pictures by foreigners, yet we take no trouble to preserve these matchless works of art, the work of our own ancestors.

There have been four great periods of destruction, each with its own characteristics. Indeed, from the Reformation down to the present day the work has gone on intermittently.

During the sixteenth century, the extreme Reformers united with those bent on plunder to rob our churches of these monuments. Brass has at all times been a valuable metal, and when religious zeal is combined with greed of gain, it is not surprising that thousands of brasses perished. The destruction of the great monastic churches brought with it of necessity the spoliation of their tombs which stood within; but even the parish churches were not safe. So keen was the thirst for plunder that the ministers of Edward VI confiscated even the church plate and the money for the poor.

Elizabeth,—all credit to her,—disapproved of such conduct and ordered that the plate should be replaced, though at whose cost is unknown; and, further, that all monuments broken down should be restored. If possible, this was to be done at the cost of those who had wrought the damage, otherwise the parish was to bear the burden.

The latter command seems to have been but slightly enforced, and there are but few examples of Elizabethan restoration of earlier monuments or brasses, though a few do exist.

During the seventeenth century, the Parliamentarians wrought tremendous havoc, but have had more than their fair share credited to them. Nearly as much destruction was wrought during the eighteenth century through neglect, and often these losses are laid to the door of the Puritans by the modern guide.

CONCLUSION

But perhaps the most lamentable devastations are those wrought in the nineteenth century. They were usually done by those who claimed to be "restoring" their parish churches. For example, while restoring a certain country church some twenty or thirty years ago, the architect found there were several old brasses which were being abominably treated. He informed a well-known firm of art metal workers, who sent down one of the partners. He found the workmen using one of the figures as a frying-pan over a wood fire in the churchyard! He rescued it, and many others which had been thrown out into the churchyard. Then he brought the matter to the notice of the incumbent, who absolutely refused to have anything to do with them, and declared that he would not have them in the church. Further, he told the partner that he could take them away. The latter hesitated to do so, and left them behind. A few days later, he received a box containing them. Not knowing what to do with them, he stored them away and forgot all about them.

Some twenty years later, they were re-discovered by his son, who showed them to some friends, and in the end he returned them to the church, suggesting that they should be restored to their proper places. He never even received an acknowledgement, but learnt later they were still lying neglected in the box.

The little value attached by many to brasses may

be judged from the fact that Gilbert Scott replaced the fine brass at St John's College, Cambridge, beneath the organ loft; and Pearson hid another away in the crypt of Truro. Often this scant respect was not shown, and they were sold as old metal, or, at best, torn from their stone matrices and fixed to a wall.

This latter is a constant trick of restorers, and should be strongly discouraged. Within the last year it has happened at Merstham, Surrey, and, indeed, hardly a year passes but it takes place somewhere. Firstly, the stone should not be removed at all, if in its original spot it marks the grave of the deceased, and this alone should be a sufficient reason for not removing it. If it must be removed and placed against the wall, the whole stone should be moved, and not merely the brass. Brass and stone are one and should not be separated. They may fitly be compared to a jewel and its setting.

Moreover, in raising them, the brasses become bent and twisted, and parts are nearly always lost. Further, if in its original matrix, one can fairly accurately judge of what is missing and, if it is desired, restore it.

Sometimes the excuse given for the removal is that it is to preserve them from the wear of people walking over them. This can be far better done by placing carpet or matting over them.

CONCLUSION

Even where only the matrix remains, it should be carefully preserved, as it is often of considerable interest and always the remnant of ancient work. They are of far more interest than a series of slabs of black and white marble or a series of modern machine-made tiles.

In some cases they might be carefully restored. The matrix gives a very faithful guide, and sometimes descriptions still exist. In the case where only part of the brass is lost, this should most certainly be done. Recently the author helped to restore an old brass at Shere, Surrey, the cost of the work being most generously borne by the Rector (Mr Hill).

John Touchet, Lord Audley, was executed on the charge of high treason by Henry VII in 1490. An altar tomb was set up in his memory about 1525. It showed a figure in armour with a marginal inscription on a chamfered edge. About 1745 the tomb was destroyed, and the top slab laid in the floor of the chancel. As the chamfered edge would thus be hidden, some person stole the brass fillet. About 1800 the lower half of the effigy was also stolen. When the church was restored in 1896, a parishioner gave the Rector a piece of the inscription which she had found hidden away in an old cottage she had recently bought. Not knowing to what figure it belonged, he fastened it to a window sill. Recently the writer drew his attention to the fact that it undoubtedly belonged to the mutilated figure, and suggested that a fresh matrix should be cut round the edge of the stone, and that the remainder of the inscription and the legs should be restored. To this he agreed, and the work was carefully executed by Messrs Gawthorp of 16, Long Acre. Fortunately the piece of inscription contained almost all the personal details save the year of Touchet's death. This was discovered from documentary evidence to be 1490. A description of the legs was also found, taken just before they were stolen. This was fortunate, as one would not otherwise have known that there was a greyhound *between* his feet. Our thanks are due to Mr Mill Stephenson for much valuable advice and information. Every care was taken to make the new work as exactly like the old in colour and engraving as possible. But to prevent deception, each new piece was marked on the back with the date, 1911, and, further, a careful rubbing was taken before the restoration, showing the old work and the matrix, and this was framed and hung in the South Porch.

The matrix of a fine cross with a prior kneeling at the foot was restored some years ago at Ely.

Where a brass is loose, it should be refixed. Palimpsests may cause some difficulty. By far the best method is to have careful electrotypes made of the reverses and fastened up in the church, and the

CONCLUSION

originals should then be permanently refixed in their matrices.

One cannot close without emphasizing the terrible destruction of these priceless works of art.

In St Albans Abbey, a few years ago, no less than 270 matrices were counted. Durham Cathedral, once paved with brasses, has not *one* left!

These matrices should be preserved, and, as yet, a complete catalogue of them has not been made. It is to be hoped that some antiquary will ere long undertake the task. There are still a great number —perhaps 6000—and often of unique interest. In several cases these slabs are older than the earliest surviving brasses. For example, the earliest of all is at St Paul's, Bedford. It is believed to commemorate Sir Simon de Beauchamp, 1208, mentioned by Leland. There was a large cross 5 ft. 9 in. × 2 ft. 6 in. springing from a plate with an inscription, and having a small shield on either side of the head. There was also a border fillet.

Again, there is a splendid matrix at Durham, now carefully protected beneath a thick carpet. It is to Bp. Beaumont, 1333, and is larger and finer than any brass now extant, measuring 15 ft. × 10 ft. As a very complete description of it exists in a sixteenth century book, it would be comparatively easy to restore it to its former magnificence. And it must have been a splendid brass! The bishop is in full canonicals and a small angel censing him on either side. He stands beneath a fine triple canopy with super-canopy and saints. The shafts contain niches with the apostles, and on either side are side shafts connected to the canopy by flying buttresses and containing twelve figures of his ancestors. There are two lions beneath his feet and a border fillet, besides other interesting details. Is it too much to hope that some day money will be forthcoming to restore it?

Though we advocate a judicious restoration, it must be *well* done, or not at all. We all know the harm that has been wrought by zealous "restorers" of our churches, and we must not allow the same evil to befall the brasses.

The right lines to follow, in the author's opinion, have already been described. The *wrong* way is to break the following rules:

(1) Never destroy any of the original brass.

(2) Never destroy the original matrix, and always let it act as a guide.

(3) Be sure and use the proper alloy. The old latten is of different alloy from the ordinary brass of modern commerce, which is much softer.

(4) Do not get an amateur or a local artist, who has had little or no experience in this kind of work,

xv] CONCLUSION 109

to do it. Go to one of the few firms which have made a special study of this kind of work. They may seem a little expensive, but in the end it is well worth the difference.

(5) If you want advice, write to the Monumental Brass Society, London, or, if you prefer it, to the author, who would always be glad to help in any way he could.

(6) See if there are any rubbings or description extant in the British Museum or elsewhere.

Perhaps this is an appropriate place at which to draw attention to the latent possibilities of a revival of brasses for modern memorials. When one reflects on the over-crowded state of some of our finest cathedrals with hideous and cumbersome monuments, the desirability of this revival becomes apparent. They would take up practically no space, and therefore would not interfere with the architecture of the building, as do the statues in Westminster Abbey. They are in keeping with the Gothic style of most of our churches. If good, they can be of considerable beauty and interest; if bad, a mat readily hides them from view.

One difficulty undoubtedly obtrudes itself, viz. modern dress. However, both Church and Army lend themselves to picturesque and fortuitous treatment. For the civilian, university gowns, mayoral and civic robes and even court dress are quite amenable to the engraver's art.

As to women's attire, a simple arrangement of veil or scarf about the head would be acceptable and dignified, in conjunction with garments of flowing and harmonious lines. Grotesque contours and eccentric mannerisms of attire would naturally be avoided. In this matter one need but follow in the steps of the old engravers.

The faces would either be portraits or not, as seemed desirable to those who had the brass laid down.

Two types might be followed :

(1) The old Gothic, with the figures recumbent, in which case the brass should be placed on the floor.

(2) The Renaissance, with the figure kneeling, as in many of the Elizabethan examples. These should be affixed to the wall. The faults of these latter are usually :

(a) Thin metal.

(b) Too much detail.

(c) Lack of depth in graving.

All these defects could be avoided to-day.

Certain modern specimens do exist, but cannot, as a rule, be placed in the front rank. An exception must be made in favour of a modern brass on the old lines laid down by Messrs Gawthorp at Islip, Northants. It is meant to replace a fifteenth century brass long since entirely vanished. A civilian and his wife, in the dress of c. 1460, stand beneath a double canopy, and the effect is most pleasing.

There is also a rather fine one to W. S. Sanders, Rector of St Nicholas, Guildford, 1901, and two in Westminster Abbey.

But so far no really fine example showing the figures in modern dress has been laid down. In the author's opinion, it is to be hoped that the art of enamelling brasses will not be restored to favour at the same time. Nor does he consider that the engraved lines should be filled in with coloured matter or black wax.

In conclusion; if even a few, by reading this little book, are persuaded to study and help to preserve the ancient relics of the past, the author will feel that it has not been written in vain.

There is undoubtedly a decided awakening of interest in the subject, but it behoves us to exert ourselves to make *all* realize how priceless are the four thousand which alone survive out of the large number (some 150,000, including inscriptions) which were at one time or another laid down.

APPENDIX

I. 1277–1327

* Sir John Daubernon, Stoke d'Abernon, Surrey, 1277.
* Sir Roger de Trumpington, Trumpington, Cambs., 1289.
d Sir Rich. de Boselyngthorpe, Buslingthorpe, Lincs., c. 1290.
d Unknown Knight, Croft, Lincs., c. 1300.
* Sir Robert de Bures, Acton, Suffolk, 1302.
* Sir Robert de Setvans, Chatham, Kent, 1306.
* Margarete de Camoys, Trotton, Sussex, c. 1310.
d Rich. de Hakebourne (priest), Merton Coll., Oxford, c. 1310.
* Archbishop Wm. de Grenefeld, York Minster, 1315.
* Sir — Fitzralph, Pebmarsh, Essex, c. 1320.
* Sir — Bacon, Gorleston, Suffolk, c. 1320.
* Joan de Cobham, Cobham, Kent, c. 1320.
  Nichol de Gore (priest), Woodchurch, Kent, c. 1320.
d A Priest, Chinnor, Oxford, c. 1320.
d Thos. de Hop (priest), Kemsing, Kent, c. 1320.
d A Priest, Wantage, Berks., c. 1320.
d John de Bladigdone and wife (civilian), demi, in cross, East Wickham, Kent, c. 1325.
* Sir John de Creke and wife, Westley Waterless, Cambs., c. 1325.
* Sir John Daubernon II, Stoke d'Abernon, Surrey, 1327.
* Sir John de Northwode and wife, Minster-in-Sheppey, Kent, c. 1330.

Nearly life-size figures are marked with a star, and d = demi.

APPENDIX

II. 1327–1399

The following is believed to be a complete list of the military brasses of this period:—

† Sir John de Cobham (with church), Cobham, Kent, 1354.
John Bodiam, Bodiam, Sussex (small), c. 1360.
* Wm. de Aldeburgh (on bracket), Aldborough, Yorks., c. 1360.
Sir Philip Peletoot, Watton, Herts., 1361.
Unknown, Gt. Berkhampstead, Herts., c. 1365.
John de Cobham, Cobham, Kent, c. 1365.
† Sir Thos. de Cobham, Cobham, Kent, 1367.
† Sir Adam de Clyfton, Methwold, Norfolk, 1367.
Thos. Cheyne, Drayton Beauchamp, Bucks., 1368.
Ralph de Knevyngton, Aveley, Essex, 1370.
† Sir John de la Pole and wife, Chrishall, Essex, c. 1370.
Unknown, Freshwater, I. o. W., c. 1370.
Sir Henry Redford and wife, Broughton, Lincs., c. 1370.
Edmund Flambard (on bracket), Harrow, Middlesex, c. 1370.
John Wybarne, Ticehurst, Sussex, c. 1370.
Thos. Stapel (Serj.-at-arms), Shopland, Essex, 1371.
Sir John de Mereworth, Mereworth, Kent, 1371.
Sir John de Foxley and two wives (on bracket), Bray, Berks., 1378.
Unknown, Calbourne, I. o. W., c. 1380.
Unknown, St Michael's, St Albans, Herts., c. 1380.
Roger de Felbrigg, Felbrigg, Norfolk, c. 1380.
†* A Dallingridge and wife, Fletching, Sussex, c. 1380.
A Quinton, Clyffe Pypard, Wilts., c. 1380.
Rich. de Feversham, Graveney, Kent, 1381.
Sir John de Argentine, Horseheath, Cambs., 1382.
† Lord Nicholas Burnell, Acton Burnell, Salop, 1382.
* Sir John Harsyck and wife, in armorial mantle, Southacre, Norfolk, 1384.

BRASSES

Regd. de Malyn and two wives, Chinnor, Oxon., 1385.
Sir Thos. de Audley, Audley, Staffs., 1385.
Esmoun de Malyn and wife, Chinnor, Oxon., 1386.
Sir Robt. de Grey, Rotherfield Grays, Oxon., 1387.
Sir Wm. de Echingham, Etchingham, Sussex, 1388.
† Sir John de Wyngefield, Letheringham, Suffolk, 1389.
Sir Andrew Louttrell, Irnham, Lincs., 1390.
John Flambard, Harrow, Middlesex, c. 1390.
Robt. Russel, Strensham, Worc., c. 1390.
† Sir Wm. Kerdeston and wife, Reepham, Norfolk, 1391.
Thos. Ld. Berkley and wife, Wootton-under-Edge, Glos., 1392.
John Gray, Chinnor, Oxon., 1392.
Sir Thos. Walsch and wife, Wanlip, Leics., 1393.
Henry English and wife, Wood Ditton, Cambs., 1393.
† Ld. Rich. Atte Lese and wife, Sheldwich, Kent, 1394.
Sir Edw. Cerne and wife, Draycott Cerne, Wilts., 1394.
Ld. Wm. de Bryene, Seal, Kent, 1395.
Sir Jn. de Quintin and wife, Brandsburton, Yorks., 1397.
John Bettesthorne, Mere, Wilts., 1398.

In this list those which are starred * show armorial jupons, and those with daggers † have canopies.

Some examples of ladies *alone*, in addition to those included in the text, are given :—

Unknown, Norbury, Staffs., c. 1350.
Joan Plessi, Quainton, Bucks., c. 1360.
Isabella Beaufo, Waterperry, Oxon., c. 1370.
A Cobham, Lingfield, Surrey, c. 1370.
Ismayne Winston, Necton, Norfolk, 1372.
Lady Margaret de Cobham, Cobham, Kent, 1375.
Lady Maud de Cobham, Cobham, Kent, 1380.
Margt. Holes, Watford, Herts., c. 1390.
Margery Wyllughby, Spilsby, Lincs., 1391.

APPENDIX 115

Lady Margaret de Cobham, Cobham, Kent, 1395.
Alianore de Bohun, Duchess of Glo'ster, Westminster Abbey, 1399.

Civilians: a selection.

Man and wife, Upchurch, Kent, demi, 1340.
Rich. Torrington and wife (fine), Gt. Berkhampstead, Herts., 1356.
John de Walden, Ashbury, Berks., demi, c. 1360.
A frankelein and a priest (fine), Shottesbrook, Berks., c. 1370.
John de Feversham and mother, Graveney, Kent, demi, c. 1370.
A frankelein, Cheam, Surrey, c. 1370.
Two Civilians, Kings Somborne, Hants., c. 1380.
Symon de Felbrigg and wife, Felbrigg, Norfolk, c. 1382.
Unknown, Hampsthwaite, Yorks., c. 1380.
John Alderburne, Lewknor, Oxon., demi, 1380.
John Corp and granddaughter, under peculiar double canopy, Stoke Fleming, Devon, 1391.
John Curteys and wife, under double canopy (a woolman), Wimington, Beds., 1391.
Unknown, Temple Church, Bristol, 1396.
Walter Pescod (wife lost) under fine double triple canopy, Boston, Lincs., 1398.

III. 1400–1453

(i)

Sir Geo. Felbrigg, Playford, Suffolk, 1400.
Sir Thos. Massingberd and wife, Gunby St Peter, Lincs. (double canopy), c. 1400.
Unknown (triple canopy), Laughton, Lincs., c. 1400.
Thos. de Beauchamp, E. of Warwick, and wife, St Mary's, Warwick, 1401.

BRASSES

Sir Nich. Dagworth, Blickling, Norfolk, 1401.
Sir Wm. Fienlez, Hurstmonceaux, Sussex (canopy), 1402.
Sir Reg. Braybrok, Cobham, Kent (canopy), 1405.
Sir Roger Drury and wife, Rougham, Suffolk, 1405.
Sir Nich. Hawberk, Cobham, Kent (canopy), 1407.
Sir Wm. Bagot and wife, Baginton, Warwick, 1407.
Wm. Snayth, Esq. and wife, Addington, Kent (double canopy), 1409.
Lord Bourgchier and two wives, Halstead, Essex, 1409.
Wm., Lord Willoughby d'Eresby and wife, Spilsby, Lincs. (double triple canopy), 1410.
Sir Thos. Burton and wife, Little Casterton, Rutland, c. 1410.
Sir Robt. Swynborne, Little Horkesley, Essex (triple canopy), 1412. (See below.)
Robt., Lord Ferrers and wife, Merevale Abbey, Warwick, 1412.
Sir Geo. Felbrigg and Sir Wm. Bagot (1400) at Playford in Suffolk, (1407) at Baginton, Warwick, wear armorial jupons.

The Order of the Garter is found at Exeter Cathedral, 1409, Felbrigg, Norfolk, 1416, and Trotton, Sussex, 1419. These wear the Garter only. Perhaps at Tattershall, Lincs., 1455, and certainly at Little Easton, Essex, 1483, both Garter and Mantle are worn. Finally, Thos. Bullen, Hever, Kent, 1538, wears the full insignia. There is a palimpsest (see *Palimpsests*) fragment c. 1530 showing part of the Mantle and Garter at Holy Trinity, Chester.

Transitional examples:—

Sir Reg. de Cobham, Lingfield, Surrey, 1403.
John Hanley and two wives, Dartmouth, Devon, 1408 (triple canopy).
Thos. Seintleger, Otterden, Kent, 1408.

APPENDIX 117

John Wylcotes and wife (canopy), Gt. Tew, Oxon., 1410.
Sir Thos. Swynborne and father (under double triple canopy), Little Horkesley, Essex, 1412.

(ii) Typical Lancastrian examples.

Sir Jn. Routh and wife (with S.S.), Routh, Yorks., c. 1410.
Thos. de Crewe and wife, Wixford, Warw. (canopy and additional badges), 1411.
Geof. Fransham, Gt. Fransham, Norfolk (canopy), 1414.
Sir Jn. Phelip, Walter Cookesey, and wife (S.S.) (triple canopy), Kidderminster, Worc., 1415.
Sir Jn. Erpingham, Erpingham, Norfolk, c. 1415. (He built the Erpingham Gate, Norwich Cathedral.)
Sir Thos. de Skelton and two wives, Hinxton, Cambs., 1416.
Sir Symon Felbrigge, K.G., and wife (canopy), Felbrigg, Norfolk, 1416.
Lord Thos. Camoys, K.G., and wife (double canopy), Trotton, Sussex, 1419.
John Doreward and wife, Bocking, Essex, 1420.
Sir Wm. Calthorpe (S.S.), Burnhamthorpe, Norfolk (canopy and super-canopy), 1420.
Peter Halle and wife, Herne, Kent, c. 1420.
Sir John Lysle, Thruxton, Hants. (triple canopy), died 1407, engraved c. 1425.
John Lowe, Battle, Sussex, 1426.
Sir John de Brewys, Wiston, Sussex (additional scrolls), 1426
Lord Thos. de Straunge (S.S.), Wellesbourne, Warw., 1426.
John Norwiche and wife, Yoxford, Suffolk, 1428.
Wm. Harwedon and wife, Gt. Harrowden, Northants., 1433.
Wm. Scot, Brabourn, Kent, 1434.
Thos. Wideville, Esq. and two wives (triple canopy), Bromham, Beds., c. 1435.
Thos. Chaucer and wife, Ewelme, Oxon., 1436.
Sir John Harpedon, Westminster Abbey, 1437.

(iii) Changes.

Sir John Leventhrop and wife, Sawbridgeworth, Herts., 1433.
Sir Rich. Delamere and wife, Hereford Cathedral (canopy), 1435.
John Weston, Albury, Surrey (headless), 1440.
Man in Armour, Arkesden, Essex, c. 1440.
Sir Wm. Wadham and wife, Ilminster, Somerset, c. 1440 (double triple canopy and super-canopy).
Reg. Barantyn, Chalgrove, Oxon., 1441.
Thos. de St Quintin, Harpham, Yorks., 1445.
Sir Chris. Baynham and Wife, Newland, Glos., c. 1448.

(iv) Transitional.

Sir Wm. Etchingham, wife and son (triple canopy), Etchingham, Sussex, 1444.
John Gaynesford, Crowhurst, Surrey, 1450.
Walter Grene, Hayes, Middlesex, c. 1450.
Unknown, Isleworth, Middlesex, c. 1450.
Thos. Reynes and wife, Marston Mortayne, Beds., 1451.
Sir John Bernard and wife (S.S.), Isleham, Cambs. (double canopy), 1451.

Woolmen and Civilians: a selection.

A Woolman and wife and several others, Northleach, Glos., c. 1400.
A Civilian and wife and several others, Ore, Sussex, c. 1400.
Rich. Martyn and wife, Dartford, Kent (double canopy), 1402.
Robt. de Haitfield and wife, Owston, Yorks., 1409.
Nich. Atte Heel, Chinnor, Oxford, c. 1410.
Hugo de Gondeby, Tattershall, Lincs., 1411.
Thos. Fayreman and wife, St Albans Abbey (Woolman), 1411.
John Lyndewode and wife (double canopy), Lyndewode, Lincs., 1419 (Woolman), and others.
Harry Hawes (English Inscription), Arreton, I. o. W., c. 1430.

APPENDIX 119

Nich. Carrew and wife, Beddington, Surrey, 1432.
Simon Seeman, Barton-on-Humber (Vintner), 1433.
Robt. Skern and wife, Kingston, Surrey, 1437.
John Bacon and wife (Woolman), All Hallows, Barking, 1437.
Wm. Markeby and wife, St Bartholomew the Less, London, 1439.
Robt. Page and wife (double canopy), Cirencester, Glos., 1440.
John Hicchecok, Ampthill, Beds. (Woolman), 1450.
Laurence Pygott and wife, Dunstable, Beds. (Woolman), 1450.
John Yonge and wife, Chipping Norton, Oxon. (Woolman), 1451.
Edm. Mille and wife, Pulborough, Sussex, 1452.

Judges : complete list.

Sir Jn. Cassy and wife, Deerhurst, Glos. (canopy), 1400.
Sir Hugh de Holes (mutilated), Watford, Herts., 1415.
Wm. de Lodyngton, Gunby, Lincs. (canopy), 1419.
Rich. Norton and wife (worn), Wath, Yorks., 1420.
Jn. Staverton (mutilated), Eyke, Suffolk, c. 1430.
Jn. Martyn and wife, Graveney, Kent (double canopy), 1436.
Sir Jn. Juyn, St Mary, Redcliff, Bristol, 1439.
Jn. Cottusmore and wife, Brightwell Baldwin, Oxon., 1439.

IV. 1453–1485

About 70 knights still exist, from which the following are selected :—

Robert Staunton and wife, Castle Donington, Leics. (canopy), 1458.
Sir Thos. Shernborne and wife, Shernborne, Norfolk, 1458.
Sir Robt. del Bothe and wife, Wilmslow, Cheshire, 1460.
Rich. Quatremayns, wife and son, Thame, Oxon., c. 1460.
Wm. Prelatte, Esq. and two wives, Cirencester, Glos., 1462.
Robt. Eyr and wife, Hathersage, Derbys., 1463.
John Threel and wife, Arundel, Sussex, 1463.

BRASSES

John Ansty, Stow-cum-Quy, Camb., c. 1465.
Hen. Paris, Hildersham, Cambs. (canopy), 1466.
Rich. Ask and wife, Aughton, Yorks., 1466.
Sir Thos. Strathum and two wives, Morley, Derbys., 1470.
Unknown, Holbrook, Suffolk, 1470.
Robt. Wotton and wife, Addington, Kent, 1470.
Robt. Ingylton and three wives, Thornton, Bucks., 1472 (fine under quadruple canopy).
Wm. Fitz-William and widow, Sprotborough, Yorks., 1474.
Sir Antony Grey, St Albans Abbey, 1480.
Sir Thos. Vaughan (mutilated), Westminster Abbey, 1483.
Thos. Peyton and two wives, Isleham, Cambs., 1484.
Sir Thos. Brewes and wife, Fressingfield, Suffolk (engraved), c. 1485.

Ladies' Dress.

A few examples are given :—

Agnes Molyngton (widow), Dartford, Kent, 1454.
Eliz. Dencourt, Upminster, Essex (heraldic), 1455.
Cecilie Boleyn (maid), Blickling, Norfolk, 1458.
Jane Keriell, Ash-next-Sandwich, Kent (peculiar head-dress), c. 1460.
Christine Phelip, Herne, Kent (peculiar), 1470.
Marg. Elmes, All Saints, Stamford, Lincs., 1471.
Joan Haselden, Oxted, Surrey, 1480.
Margery Clopton and Alice Harleston, Long Melford, Suffolk (heraldic), c. 1480.

Lawyers.

(a) Judges.

Nich. Assheton and wife, Callington, Cornwall, c. 1465.
Sir Peter Arderne and wife, Latton, Essex, 1467.
Sir Wm. Yelverton and wife, Rougham, Norfolk, c. 1470 (in armour, mantle, coif and hood, and wearing collar of roses and suns).

APPENDIX 121

Sir Wm. Laken, Bray, Berks. (wife lost), 1475.
Sir Rich. Byngham and wife, Middleton, Warw., 1476.
Sir Thos. Urswyk and wife, Dagenham, Essex, 1479.
Sir Thos. Billyng and wife, Wappenham, Northants., 1481.
Brian Rouclyff, Cowthorpe, Yorks. (wife lost), 1494.

The last may be included here, as his costume belongs more nearly to the Yorkist than to the Tudor period. It was a most interesting brass, including the model of the church, which he founded, and a bier commemorating his uncle. It had also a double canopy. Several of the most interesting features remain, but the rest was stolen a few years after Waller described it in 1841.

(b) Notaries.

Unknown, Gt. Chart, Kent, c. 1470.
Unknown, St Mary's Tower, Ipswich, c. 1475.
Barth. Willesdon, Willesdon, Middlesex (peculiar), 1492.
Unknown, St Mary's Tower, Ipswich, 1506.
Unknown, New College, Oxford, c. 1510.

Other Civilians.

Jn. Fortey (Woolman), Northleach, Glos. (canopy), 1458, and others.
Jn. Browne and wife (Woolman), All Saints', Stamford, Lincs. (canopy), c. 1460.
Edward Courtenay, Ch. Ch. Cath., Oxon., c. 1460.
John Lethenard and wife, Chipping Campden, Glos., 1467.
Jn. Waliston and two wives (a smith), Chenies, Bucks., 1469.
Jn. Wynter (mayor), St Margt., Canterbury, 1470.
Ralph Segrim and wife (mayor), St John, Maddermarket, Norwich, 1472.
John Feld (Woolman), Standon, Herts., 1477.
Thos. Rowley and wife (sheriff), St John's, Bristol, 1478.
John Cobleigh and two wives, Chittlehampton, Devon, 1480.

BRASSES

Jn. Jay and wife (sheriff), St Mary, Redcliff, Bristol, c. 1480.
Robt. Lytton and wife, Tideswell, Derbys., 1483.

At Stopham, Sussex, there is an interesting series of brasses to officials of Arundel Castle, c. 1460 and onwards.

V

There are about 450 brasses of mass priests, of which the following are worthy of note.

Those over 3 ft. long are marked with a star :—

*St Lawrence de St Maur, Higham Ferrers (with canopy), Northants., 1337.
*John de Grovehurst, Horsmonden, Kent (with canopy), c. 1340.
Wm. de Herleston, Sparsholt, Berks., c. 1360.
Unknown, with chalice, North Mimms, Herts., c. 1360.
Esmund de Burnedissh, Brundish, Suffolk, c. 1360.
*Simon de Wenslagh, with chalice, Wensley, Yorks., c. 1360.
*John Seys, West Hanney, Berks., c. 1370.
*Unknown, Shottesbrook, Berks., with franklin (under double canopy), c. 1370.
Unknown, Stoke-in-Teignhead, Devon, c. 1370.
Wm. de Lound, Althorpe, Lincs., c. 1370.
Robt. Levee, Hayes, Middlesex, c. 1370.
*Peter de Lacy, Northfleet, Kent, 1375.
Unknown, Beachamwell St Mary, Norfolk, c. 1385.
*John de Swynsteade, Ashridge House, Herts., formerly at Edlesborough (with part of canopy), 1395.
Unknown, with chalice, Stanford-on-Soar, Leic., c. 1400.
Wm. de Thorp, West Wickham, Kent, 1407.
John Mordon, Emberton, Bucks., c. 1410.
*Rich. Bayly, Hoo St Werburgh, Kent, 1412.
Robt. Scarclyf, Shere, Surrey, 1412.
Robt. Fyn, Little Easton, Essex, c. 1420.
Robt. Willardsey, St Nicholas, Warwick, 1424.

APPENDIX 123

Adam Babyngton, Milton Keynes, Bucks., 1427.
Roger Godeale, with chalice, Bainton, Yorks., 1429.
Robt. Clere, Battle, Sussex, c. 1430.
Edw. Cranford, Puttenham, Surrey, 1431.
John Heyne, Yelden, Beds., 1434.
John Colt, Tansor, Northants., 1440.
John Baker, Arundel, Sussex, 1445.
Rich. Goldon, with heart, Willian, Herts., 1446.
Unknown, Turweston, Bucks., c. 1450.
Roger Gery, with chalice, Whitchurch, Oxon., 1456.
Robt. Lond, with chalice, St Peter's, Bristol, 1461.
*John Spycer (?), Monkton-in-Thanet, Kent, c. 1465.
John Swetecock, Lingfield, Surrey, 1469.
Thos. Wyrley, with heart, Letchworth, Herts., 1475.
Gulfrid Bysschop (hands crossed downwards), Fulbourn, Cambs., 1477.
Unknown, with chalice, Laindon, Essex, c. 1480.
Roger Clerk, St Ethelred, Norwich, 1487.
John Balam, Blewbury, Berks., 1496.
Alex. Inglisshe, with chalice, Campsey Ash, Suffolk, 1504.
Thos. Warner, Soulderne, Oxon., 1508.
Thos. Symons, Gt. Greenford, Middlesex, c. 1515.
John Wright, with chalice, Clothall, Herts., 1519.
Wm. Grey, with chalice, Evershot, Dorset, 1524.
John ap Meredyth, with chalice, Bettws, Montgy., 1531.
Wm. Wardsworth, with chalice, Betchworth, Surrey, 1533.
Wm. Harman, with chalice, Eton College, Bucks., 1535.
Robt. Hanson (small), Chalfont St Peter, Bucks., 1545.

In a few brasses the stole or maniple is omitted. These are probably the work of careless local engravers. Examples are found at Dronfield, Derby, 1399; Clothall, Herts., 1404; Newton Bromshold, Northants., 1426; Sparham, Norfolk, 1490; Blockley, Worc., c. 1500; Laindon, Essex, c. 1510; and elsewhere.

BRASSES

Chalice Brasses.

(a) Yorkshire.

Rich. Kendale, Ripley, 1429.
Peter Johnson, Bishop Burton, 1460.
Wm. Langton, St Michael Spurriergate, York, 1466.
Thos. Clarell, St Peter's, Leeds, 1469.

(b) Norfolk.

John Smyth, St Giles, Norwich, 1499.
Rich. Grene, Hedenham, 1502.
Robt. Northen, Buxton, 1508.
Rich. Louhouwys, Surlingham, 1513.
Edmund Ward, North Walsham, 1519.
Wm. Westow, Little Walsingham, c. 1520, and several others.

There are but few elsewhere, such as:

Robt. Wodehowse, Holwell, Beds., 1515.
Thos. Elys, Shorne, Kent, 1519.
Thos. King, Renham, Suffolk, 1523.
Unknown, Gazeley, Suffolk, 1530.

Cassock alone.

Thos. Awmarle, Cardynham, Cornwall, c. 1400.
Unknown (kn.), peculiar, Aspley Guise, Beds., c. 1410.
John Lewys (kn.), Quainton, Bucks., 1422.
Unknown, Cirencester, Glos., c. 1480.
Unknown, North Creake, Norfolk, c. 1500.
Rich. Bethel, Shorwell, I. o. W., 1518.
John Yslyngton, with chalice, Cley, Norfolk, c. 1520.
Wm. Lawnder (kn.), Northleach, Glos., c. 1530.

Almuce.

John Morys, First Warden, Winchester College, Hants., 1413.
Wm. Whyte, Arundel, Sussex, 1419.
John Huntington, Warden, Manchester Cathedral, 1458.
Robt. Brerely, Billingham, Durham, 1480.
Thos. Barker, Eton College, Bucks. (fellow), 1489.
Canon Thos. Teylar, Byfleet, Surrey, 1489.
Wm. Fordmell, Bordon, Kent, 1490.
Thos. Parker, Dean, Beds., 1501.
Henry Bost (Provost), Eton College, Bucks., 1503.
Ralph Elcock, Tong, Salop, 1510.
John Fynexs, Archdeacon of Sudbury, St Mary's, Bury St Edmunds, 1514.
Wm. Goberd, B.A., Archdeacon, Magdalen College, Oxford, 1515.
Robt. Honywode, LL.D., quadrilateral plate, St George's Chapel, Windsor (peculiar), 1522.
Rich. Adams, with chalice, East Maling, Kent, 1522.
Robt. Hacombleyn (Provost), King's College, Cambridge, 1528.
Robt. Sutton (Dean), St Patrick's Cath., Dublin (quadrilateral plate, peculiar), 1528.
Geoff. Fyche (Dean), St Patrick's Cath., Dublin (quadrilateral plate, peculiar), 1537.
Jas. Coorthopp (Dean of Peterborough), Christ Ch., Oxford, 1557.
Robt. Brassie, S.T.P., Provost, King's College, Cambridge, 1558.

The Cope: a selection.

Wm. de Rothwelle, Rothwell, Northants. (curious), 1361.
John de Campden, St Cross, Winchester, 1382.
Nich. de Luda, Cottingham, Yorks., 1383.
Wm. de Fubburne, Fulbourn, Cambs. (canopy), 1391.
Math. de Asscheton, Shillington, Beds., 1400.
John Sleford, Balsham, Cambridge, 1401.

BRASSES

Rich. Malford, New College, Oxford, 1403.
Hen. de Codryngton, Bottesford, Leic. (canopy), 1404.
Wm. Langeton, Exeter Cathedral (kn.), 1403.
Simon Bache, Knebsworth, Herts., 1414.
John Prophete, Ringwood, Hants., 1416.
Thos. Patteslie, Gt Shelford, Cambs., 1418.
Robt. Wyntryngham, Cotterstock, Northants., 1420.
Thos. Harlyng, Pulborough, Sussex, 1423.
Rich. Cassey, Tredington, Worcs., 1427.
Hen. Mowbray, Upwell, Norfolk, 1428.
John Mapilton, Broadwater, Sussex (canopy), 1432.
John Stanwey, Hereford Cathedral, 1434.
Wm. Prestwyk, Warbleton, Sussex, 1436.
Jn. Lovelle, St Geo., Canterbury (no almuce), 1438.
Simon Marcheford, Harrow, Middlesex, 1442.
Robt. Arthur, Chartham, Kent, 1454.
John Blodwell, Balsham, Cambs., 1462.
Hen. Sever, Merton College, Oxford, 1471.
Wm. Langley, Buckland, Herts. (with chalice), 1478.
Wm. Gisburne, Kirby Wharfe, Yorks., 1480.
Wm. Malster, Girton, Cambs., 1492.
Walter Hyll, New College, Oxford, 1494.
Jas. Hart, B.D., Hitchin, Herts., 1498.
Hen. Wykys, All Saints, Stamford, Lincs., 1508.
Unknown, Tattershall, Lincs., c. 1510.
Silvester Gabriel, Croydon, Surrey, 1512.
(1) Walter Hewke, D.C.L., Trinity Hall, Cambridge, 1517.
Wm. Lichfield, LL.D., Willesdon, Middlesex, 1517.
Robt. Langton, Queen's College, Oxford, 1518.
Thos. Swayn, Wooburn, Bucks., 1519.
Christopher Urswic, Hackney, Middlesex, 1521.
Wm. Boutrod, Eton College, Bucks., 1522.
Edm. Frowsetoure, Hereford Cathedral (Renais. canopy), 1536.
Wm. Styrlay, Rauceby, Lincs., 1536.

APPENDIX 127

Thos. Dalyson, Clothall, Herts. (no almuce), 1541.
John White, Winchester College, 1548.
Thos. Magnus, Sessay, Yorks., 1550.

(1) Hewke's cope was one in use at the College at the time, and a contemporary description of it still survives. It was of red samite.

Academic Dress: a selection.

Unknown in cap, Gt. Brington, Northants., c. 1340.
John Hotham, Chinnor, Oxon., demi in cap, 1361.
John Strete, M.A., in skull cap, Upper Hardres, Kent, 1405 (kneeling before bracket, see Illus.).
Eudo de la Zouch, St John's College, Cambridge, c. 1410 (large, but mutilated).
Wm. Calwe, Ledbury, Heref., sm., kn., c. 1410.
John Mottesfont, B.C.L., Lydd, Kent, 1420.
John Lowthe, New College, Oxford, in skull cap, 1427.
Priest and parents, large, Melton, Suffolk (mut. trip. canopy), 1430.
Wm. Hautryve, D.D., New College, Oxford, in skull cap, 1441, and several others.
John Darley, Herne, Kent, skull cap, c. 1450.
Wm. Snell, M.A., Boxley, Kent, 1451.
John Alnwik, M.A., Surlingham, Norfolk, 1460.
Unknown, Harrow, Middlesex, c. 1460.
Thos. Sondes, Magdalen College, Oxford, 1478, and several others.
Unknown, D.D., Little St Mary's, Cambridge, skull cap, c. 1480.
Unknown, Little Shelford, Cambs., c. 1480.
Unknown, with chalice, Barking, Essex, c. 1480.
Nich. Wotton, LL.B., Gt. St Helen's, Bishopsgate, London, 1482.
Philip Worthyn, M.A., Blockley, Worc., kn., 1488.
Geo. Rede, Fovant, Wilts., quadrilateral plate (peculiar), 1492 (he kneels before a large Annunciation).

Wm. Towne, D.D., in cap, King's College, Cambridge, 1496, and others.

Wm. Heyward, Abingdon, Berks., 1501.

David Lloyde, LL.B., and Thos. Baker, demi, All Souls, Oxford, 1510.

John Trembras, M.A., St Michael Penkevil, Cornwall, 1515.

Arthur Vernon, M.A., Tong, Salop, 1517.

John Yslington, S.T.P., Cley, Norfolk, in cap with chalice, c. 1520.

Bryan Roos, LL.D., Childrey, Berks., 1529.

Unknown, Trinity Hall, Cambridge, c. 1530.

Unknown, Queens' College, Cambridge, c. 1535.

Unknown, Christ's College, Cambridge, c. 1535.

Wm. Bill, Westminster Abbey, 1561.

Bishops and mitred Abbots: a complete list.

Wm. de Grenefeld, Archbp. of York, York Minister, 1315.

John Trilleck, Bp. of Hereford, Hereford Cathedral (canopy), 1360.

Thos. Delamere, Abbot of St Albans, St Albans, c. 1360 (very fine foreign work, canopy, etc.).

Robt. Wyvil, Bp. of Salisbury, Salisbury Cathedral (peculiar), 1375.

Unknown, Adderley, Salop, c. 1390.

John de Waltham, Bp. of Salisbury, Westminster Abbey (with fine but mutilated canopy), 1395.

Robt. de Waldeby, Archbp. of York, Westminster Abbey (canopy), 1397.

Abbot Moote (lower half), St Albans Abbey, 1401.

Thos. Cranley, Archbp. of Dublin, New College, Oxford (canopy), 1417.

John Bowthe, Bp. of Exeter, East Horsley, Surrey, 1478 (small, side view).

Rich. Bell, Bp. of Carlisle, Carlisle Cathedral (worn, canopy), 1496.

APPENDIX 129

John Estney, Abbot of Westminster, Westminster Abbey, patron of Caxton (canopy), 1498.
Unknown Archbp., Edenham, Lincs., c. 1500.
Jas. Stanley, Bp. of Ely, Manchester Cathedral, 1515.
John Yong, Titular Bp. of Callipolis (headless), New College, Oxford, c. 1525.
Thos. Goodryke, Bp. of Ely, Ely Cathedral, 1554.
John Bell, Bp. of Worcester, St James's, Clerkenwell, 1556.
Robt. Pursglove, Suffragan Bp. of Hull, Tideswell, Derbys., 1579.

VI

Monastic brasses.

A Monk, Watton, Herts., c. 1370.
The head of a Nun, St Mary's, Kilburn, c. 1380.
The Duchess of Gloucester, Vowess, Westminster Abbey (canopy), 1399.
Joan Clopton, Vowess, Quinton, Glos., c. 1430.
Thos. Neolond, Cluniac Prior of Lewes, Cowfold, Sussex (canopy), 1433.
Dame Maria Gore, Prioress, Nether Wallop, Hants., 1436.
Geof. Langley, Benedictine Prior of Horsham St Faith, St Lawrence, Norwich, 1437
John Pyke, Friar, Denham, Bucks. (palimpsest), c. 1440.
A Nun, daughter of a Lady, c. 1440, on reverse of inscription to Nich. Suttherton, St John, Maddermarket, Norwich.
A Benedictine Monk, St Albans Abbey, c. 1450.
Wm. Jernemut, Monk, demi, c. 1460, on reverse of Alice Swane (1540), Halvergate, Norfolk.
Martin Forester, Monk, demi, on a *lectern*, Yeovil, Somerset, c. 1460.
Robt. Beauver, Benedictine Monk, St Albans Abbey, c. 1470.
A Benedictine Monk, demi, St Albans Abbey, c. 1470.

130 BRASSES

An Abbot (or Bishop), one of the children of Wm. Lucas, Wendensloft, Essex, c. 1470.

A Nun, one of the children of Sir Thos. Urswyk, Dagenham, Essex, 1479.

A Nun, one of the children of Thos. Mountford, Hornby, Yorks., 1489.

A Nun, one of the children of Sir Thos. Barnardiston, Gt. Cotes, Lincs., 1503.

Juliana Amyell, Vowess, Witton, Norfolk, c. 1505.

John Norton, with cope and crozier, South Creake, Norfolk, 1509.

A Monk and a Nun, among children of John Hampton, Minchinhampton, Glos., c. 1510.

Rich. Bewfforeste, Augustinian Abbot of Dorchester, Dorchester, Oxon., c. 1510.

John Stodeley, Augustinian Canon of St Frideswide's, Oxford, Over Winchendon, Bucks., 1515.

Joan Braham, Vowess, Frenze, Norfolk, 1519.

Thos. Rutlond, Sub Prior, St Albans Abbey, 1521.

Dame Eliz. Herwy, Benedictine Abbess, Elstow, Beds., c. 1525.

Joan Cook, Vowess, St Mary de Crypt, Glos., 1529.

Susan Kyngeston, Vowess, Shalston, Bucks., 1540.

Dame Agnes Jordon, Abbess of Sion, Denham, Bucks., c. 1540.

John Lawrence, Benedictine Abbot of Ramsey, Burwell, Camb. (palimpsest), 1542.

Marg. Dely, Nun, Treasurer of Sion, Isleworth, Middlesex, 1561.

It is believed that this includes all those brasses which can in any way be regarded as monastic, and one or two of these are doubtful. The most complete series are those of the Benedictines at St Albans.

Palimpsests engraved on back.

(a) From English Churches: a selection.

St Lawrence, Reading, 1538 (Walt. Barton). *Rev.* parts of brass of Sir John Popham, 1463.

Hedgerley, Bucks., 1540 (Bulstrode). *Rev.* various parts of abbot, etc., c. 1312–1530.

Taplow, Bucks., 1540 (Manfelde). *Rev.* eight pieces, c. 1470–1490.

Halvergate, Norf., 1540 (Swane). *Rev.* bust of Wm. Jernemut (monk), c. 1460.

Tolleshunt Darcy, Essex, c. 1540 (a lady). *Rev.* part of abbot, c. 1400.

Upminster, Essex, c. 1540 (a civilian). *Rev.* part of abbot, c. 1410.

Odiham, Hants., c. 1540 (a knight). *Rev.* several pieces, c. 1460.

Cheam, Surrey, 1542 (Fromondes). *Rev.* several pieces, c. 1500.

Holy Trinity, Chester, 1545 (Gee). *Rev.* part of Garter knight, c. 1530.

All Hallows, Barking, London, 1546 (Thynne). *Rev.* several pieces, c. 1510–1530.

Winchester College, 1548 (White). *Rev.* part of a widow, c. 1440.

Manchester Cathedral, 1548 (Ordsall). *Rev.* a lady, c. 1450.

Sessay, Yorks., 1550 (Magnus). *Rev.* several pieces, c. 1450.

Cobham, Surrey, c. 1550 (a knight). *Rev.* a priest, c. 1510.

Binfield, Berks., 1558 (Turner). *Rev.* part of abbot, c. 1420.

St John Maddermarket, Norwich, 1558 (Rugge). *Rev.* an abbot, c. 1320.

Morland, Westmorland, 1562 (Blythe). *Rev.* two knights, c. 1520.

Howden, Yorks., 1621 (Dolman). *Rev.* part of civilian, c. 1520.

There are about one hundred brasses included in this type.

BRASSES

(b) From Flemish or German Brasses.

Winestead, Yorks., c. 1540 (Hildyard). *Rev.* frag. of civilian, c. 1360.

Isleworth, Middlesex, 1544 (Chase). *Rev.* saint in niche, c. 1360.

Upminster, Essex, 1545 (Wayte). *Rev.* frag. of abbot, c. 1480.

Aylesford, Kent, 1545 (Savell). *Rev.* canopy, possibly French, c. 1530.

Bayford, Herts., c. 1545 (Knighton). *Rev.* frag. of abbot, c. 1480.

Ossington, Notts., 1551 (Peckham). *Rev.* frag. of lady, etc., c. 1360.

Hadleigh, Suffolk, c. 1560 (Taillor). *Rev.* civilian and angel, c. 1500.

Westerham, Kent, 1563 (Potter). *Rev.* column and shield, c. 1530.

St Peter Mancroft, Norwich, 1568 (Rede). *Rev.* civilian, c. 1500.

Haseley, Warw., 1573 (Throkmorton). *Rev.* canopy work, c. 1390.

Constantine, Cornwall, 1574 (Gerveys). *Rev.* man in armour, c. 1375.

Harrow, Middlesex, 1574 (Frankishe). *Rev.* border and lady, c. 1360 and c. 1370.

St Peter-in-the-East, Oxford, 1574 (Atkinson). *Rev.* canopy, c. 1520.

British Museum, fr. Wimbish, Essex, 1575 (fragment). *Rev.* marginal inscription, c. 1420.

Cookham, Berks., 1577 (Moore). *Rev.* head and background, etc., c. 1380 and c. 1480.

Wardour Castle, Wilts., c. 1577 and 1578 (Arundell). *Rev.* part of saint, canopy, etc., 1374.

APPENDIX

Yealmpton, Devon, 1580 (Copleston). *Rev.* head, saint, etc., c. 1460.
Holme-next-Sea, Norfolk, 1582 (Strickland). *Rev.* canopy, c. 1400.
Margate, Kent, 1582 (Flitt). *Rev.* border, c. 1400.

(c) Shop wastes etc.

A priest, Temple Ch., Bristol, c. 1460. *Rev.* lady, c. 1460.
A lady, Ampton, Suffolk, c. 1490. *Rev.* lady, c. 1470.
A lady (demi) on bracket, c. 1360. *Rev.* cross-legged knight, c. 1300. At Clifton Campville, Staffs.
Thos. and Isabel Englysche, 1525, Ipsden, Oxon. *Rev.* a lady and inscription, c. 1420.

VII
Early Tudor Canopies.

The following are remarkably fine :

Winwick, Lancs., triple, 1492.
Westminster (Estney), triple, 1498.
Hunstanton, Norf. (with saints), triple, 1506.
Wyvenhoe, Essex, triple, 1507.
Ardingly, Sussex, small, double, c. 1500. Illustrated.
Ardingly, Sussex, double (only upper half), 1504.
Hillingdon, Middlesex, double, 1509.
Little Wenham, Suffolk, double, 1514.
Faversham, Kent, double, 1533.

Early Tudor armour (still showing Yorkist characteristics): a selection.

Jn. Bohun and wife, Latton, Essex, c. 1485.
Edm. Clere and wife, Stokesby, Norfolk, 1488.
Nich. Gaynesford and wife, Carshalton, Surrey, c. 1490.
Rich. Curzon and wife, Kedlestone, Derbyshire, 1496.
Rich. Culpeper and wife (canopy), Ardingly, Sussex, 1504.

134 BRASSES

Sir Humphrey Stanley, Westminster Abbey, 1505.
Willm. Viscount Beaumont, Wyvenhoe, Essex (very fine, with triple canopy), 1507.

Typical.

Jn., Lord le Strange and wife, Hillingdon, Middlesex (double canopy), 1509.
Jn. Leventhorp, Gt. St Helen's, Bishopsgate, London, 1510.
Thos. Pekham and wife, Wrotham, Kent, 1512.
Jn. Ackworth and two wives, Luton, Beds., 1513.
Sir Jn. Danvers and wife, Dauntsey, Wilts., 1514.
Thos. Broke (Serjeant-at-arms) and wife, Ewelme, Oxon., 1518.
Philip Chatwyn (gent. usher), Alvechurch, Worc., 1524.
Sir Edw. Grey and two wives, Kinver, Staffs., 1528.
Sir Thos. Brooke, Ld. Cobham and wife, Cobham, Kent, 1529.
John Borell (Serjeant-at-arms), Broxbourne, Herts., 1531.
Sir Thos. Bullen, Hever, Kent (in full Garter insignia), 1538.
Thos. Hatteclyff, Addington, Surrey, 1540.
Sir Robt. Dymoke, Scrivelsby, Lincs., 1545.
John Lymsey, Hackney, Middlesex, 1545.
Thos. Clere, St Mary's, Lambeth, Surrey, 1545.

Tabard brasses : a selection.

John Fitz-Lewis and four wives, Ingrave, Essex, c. 1500.
Jn. Burgoyn and wife, Impington, Cambridge, 1505.
Sir Roger le Strange, Hunstanton, Norfolk, 1506. (Very fine. On bracket within canopy which has weepers, also in tabards of arms.)
Anthy. Fetyplace, Swinbrook, Oxon., 1510.
Anthy. Hansart and wife, kn., March, Cambs., 1517.
Ly. Jane Iwarby, kn., Ewell, Surrey, 1519.
Jn. Garney and wife, kn., quadrilateral plate, Kenton, Suffolk, 1524.

APPENDIX 135

Sir Godfrey Foljambe and wife, Chesterfield, Derbys., 1529.
Ly. Cath. Howard, St Mary's, Lambeth, 1535.
A lady, Gt. St Helen's, Bishopsgate, c. 1535.
Ly. Eliz. Scroope, Wyvenhoe, Essex, 1537.
Sir Ralph Verney and wife, Aldbury, Herts. (canopy), 1546.

Babies (alone).
Rougham, Norfolk, 1510.
Chesham Bois, Bucks., c. 1520.

(With parents.)
Cranbrook, Kent, c. 1520.

Later examples :—
Pinner, Middlesex, c. 1580.
Edgeware, Middlesex, 1599.
Upper Deal, Kent, 1606.
Odiham, Hants., 1636.

Civilians : a selection.

Over 400 are extant, mostly small and often poorly engraved.

Rich. Amondesham and wife (wool merchant), Ealing, Middlesex, c. 1490 (under fine double canopy).
Sir Rich. Wakehurst and wife, Ardingley, Sussex, died 1464, engraved c. 1500.
Rich. Wenman and two wives, Witney, Oxon., 1500.
Hen. Eliot and wife, Wonersh, Surrey, 1503.
Wm. Andrew and Jn. Monkeden and their wives, Cookham, Berks., 1503.
Robt. Foster and wife (wool merchant), Mattishall, Norfolk, 1507.
Sir Wm. Grevill and wife (judge), Cheltenham, Glos., 1513.
Chris. Rawson and two wives (wool merchant), All Hallows, Barking, 1518.

Rauf. Rowlatt and two wives (wool merchant), St Albans Abbey, Herts., 1519.

Thos. Bush and wife (under double canopy) (wool merchant), Northleach, Glos., 1526.

Henry Hatche and wife (under double canopy), Faversham, Kent, 1533.

Sir Anth. Fitzherbert and wife (judge), Norbury, Derbys., 1538.

Nich. Leveson and wife (wool merchant), St Andrew Undershaft, London, 1539.

Sir Walter Lake and wife (judge), Cople, Beds., 1544.

Thos. Holte and wife (judge), Aston, Warwick, 1545.

The inscriptions are chiefly in English and often quaintly spelt.

VIII

Transitional Period (1547–1558)

Men in armour: a selection.

(a) Without tabards.

Sir Humphrey Stafford and wife, Blatherwycke, Northants., 1548.

Thos. Giffard, Twyford, Bucks., 1551.

Rich. Fermer and wife, Easton Neston, Northants., 1552.

Sir Jn. Hampden and two wives, Gt. Hampden, Bucks., 1553.

Nich. Saunders and wife, Charlwood, Surrey, 1553.

Robt. Bulkeley and wife, quadrilateral plate, Cople, Beds., 1556.

(b) With tabards.

The brasses are usually small and badly engraved.

John Latton and wife, Blewbury, Berks., 1548.

Sir Humphrey Style and two wives, Beckenham, Kent, 1552.

Ly. Jane Guyldeford, Chelsea, Middlesex, 1555.

Henry Hobart, Loddon, Norfolk, 1561.

Sir John Tregonwell, Milton Abbey, Dorset, 1565.

APPENDIX

IX. 1558–1625.

A few examples are given below, the earlier, up to about 1575, are in the Transitional style, the later in the "tasset" armour.

Jn. Colby and wife, Brundish, Suffolk, 1560.
Sir Jn. Arundell and two wives, Stratton, Cornwall, 1561.
Geo. Medley and wife, Tiltey Abbey, Essex, 1562.
Sir Wm. Molyneux and two wives, Sefton, Lancs., 1568.
Jn. Clavell and two wives, Knowle, Dorset, 1572.
Thos. Higate and wife, Hayes, Middlesex, 1576.
Thos. Shurley and wife, Isfield, Sussex, 1579.
Rowland Lytton and two wives, Knebworth, Herts., 1582.
John Wingfield, Easton, Suffolk, 1584.
Thos. Carewe, Haccombe, Devon, 1586.
Thos. Stoughton, St Martin's, Canterbury, 1591.
Humphrey Brewster, Wrentham, Suffolk, 1593.
Jn. Clippesby and wife, Clippesby, Norfolk, 1594.
Edw. Leventhorp and wife, Sawbridgeworth, Herts., c. 1600.
Christopher Septvans and wife, Ash-next-Sandwich, Kent, 1602.
Thos. Windham, Felbrigg, Norfolk, 1608.
Rich. Barttelot and two wives, Stopham, Sussex, 1614.
Nich. Wadham and wife, Ilminster, Somerset, 1618.
Sir Clem. Edmonds and wife, Preston Deanery, Northants., 1622.

Civilians.

A few examples are given, but there are a fair number scattered up and down the country.

Sir Rich. Peyton and wife, Isleham, Cambs., 1574.
Wm. Dunche and wife, Little Wittenham, Berks., quadrilateral plate, engraved, c. 1585.
Robt. Cotton and wife, Richmond, Surrey, 1591.
Walter Bailey, New Coll., Oxford, 1592.

Jn. Martin and wife, Barton, Cambs., c. 1593.
Jn. Tedcastle and wife, Barking, Essex, 1596.
Jacob Verzelini and wife, Downe, Kent, 1607.
Anth. Cooke, Yoxford, Suffolk, 1613.
Rich. Gadburye and wife, Eyworth, Beds., 1624.

The York school of brasses will be referred to later; they include among others:—

Eliz. Fynes, York Minster, 1585.
James Cotrel, York Minster, 1595.
Robert Askwith, St Crux, York, 1597.

Clergy.

Jn. Fenton, Priest and Vicar, Coleshill, Warwick, 1566.
Patrick Fearne and wife, Parson, Sandon, Essex, c. 1580.
Jn. Garbrand, D.D., Parson, quadrilateral plate, N. Crawley, Bucks., 1589.
Edw. Leeds, LL.D., Rector, Croxton, Cambs., 1589.
Vincent Huffam and wife, Priest, St James, Dover, c. 1590.
Griffin Lloyd and wife, Chevening, Kent, 1596.
Wm. Lucas, M.A., Parson, Clothall, Herts., 1602.
Jn. Metcalfe, Stonham Aspall, Suffolk, 1606.
Jn. Burton, Rector, kn., Burgh St Margaret, Norfolk, 1608.
Isaiah Bures, M.A., Pastor, sm., kn., Northolt, Middlesex, 1610.
Peter Winder, Curate, Whitchurch, Oxon., 1610.
Humphrey Tyndall, Dean, Ely Cathedral (fine), 1614.
Jn. Wythines, D.D., Dean, Battle, Sussex, 1615.
Hen. Airay, Provost, Queen's Coll., Oxford, 1616.
Wm. Palke and wife, Minister, High Halstow, Kent, 1618.
Hugh Johnson (in pulpit), Vicar, Hackney, Middlesex, 1618.
Andrew Willet, D.D., Minister, Barley, Herts., 1621.

APPENDIX

X. 1625–1660.

Of other knights in armour than the illustration, the following are noteworthy:

Simon Mayne and wife, Dinton, Bucks., 1628.
Sir Jn. Arundel and wife, St Columb, Cornwall, c. 1630.
Christopher Playters, Sotterley, Suffolk, c. 1630.
Edm. Sawyer and wife, quadrilateral plate, Kettering, Northants., 1631.
Rich. Bugges and two wives, Harlow, Essex, 1636.
Wm. Penn and wife, Penn, Bucks., 1638.
Jn. Boscawen, quadrilateral plate, St Michael Penkevil, Cornwall, c. 1640.
Wm. Strode and wife, quadrilateral plate, Shepton Mallet, Somerset, 1649.

Civilians.

The following are characteristic examples:

Thos. Holl, Heigham, Norfolk, 1630.
Rich. Chiverton and wife, Quethiock, Cornwall, 1631.
Robt. Chambers, Swaffham Priory, Cambs., 1638.
Geo. Coles and two wives, St Sepulchre's, Northampton, 1640.
John Moorwood and wife, quadrilateral plate, Bradfield, near Ecclesfield, Yorks., 1647.

Sir John Wynne, 1620,
and his wife, 1632,
his daughter, Lady Mary Mostyn, 1658,
Sir Owen Wynne, 1660,
Kath. Lewis, 1669,
Dame Sarah Wynne, 1671.
} At Llanrwst, Denbigh. The plates are lozenge-shaped, showing usually only the bust of the deceased and are quite good portraits.

BRASSES

Clergy.

Of the clergy, only six brasses are known:

Arch. Lightfoot, rector, quadrilateral plate, Stoke Bruerne, Northants., 1625.
Thos. Stones (demi), Acle, Norfolk, 1627.
Wm. Procter, rector, Upper Boddington, Northants., 1627.
Maurice Hughes, vicar, Abergavenny, Monm., 1631.
Edw. Nayler and wife, kn., Bigby, Lincs., 1642.
Rice, Jem, rector, Husbands Bosworth, Leics., 1648.

In three cases bishops are commemorated by a mitre:

Arthur Lake, Bp. of Bath and Wells, Wells Cath., 1626.
John Prideaux, Bp. of Worcester, Bredon, Worc., 1650.
Henry Ferne, Bp. of Chester, Westminster Abbey, 1661.

Commonwealth Civilians and Women.

Bonham Faunce and two wives, Cliffe, Kent, 1652.
Jn. Davids, Haverfordwest, Pembrokes., 1654.
Anne Cary (a child), Clovelly, Devon, 1655.
Thos. Carewe and wife, quadrilateral plate, Haccombe, Devon, 1656.
Thos. Lawe (mayor), demi, Boston, Lincs., 1657.
Mary Hall, Sheriff Hutton, Yorks., 1657.
Lady Mary Mostyn, Llanrwst, Denbigh, 1658.
Rich. Breton and wife, Barwell, Leics., 1659.

XI. 1660–1773.

John Harris and wife, Milton, Cambs., 1660.
The Llanrwst series.
Philip Tenison, S.T.P., in shroud, Bawburg, Norfolk, 1660.
Mary Thorne and three daughters, St Mary, Bedford, 1663.
Robt. Shiers, Gt. Bookham, Surrey, 1668.
Shrouded Effigy on tomb, Thornton Watlass, Yorks., 1669.

APPENDIX 141

Nich. Toke in armour and three daughters kneeling, Gt. Chart, Kent, 1680.
Edm. West, Serjeant-at-law, in armour, and wife, quadrilateral plate, Marsworth, Bucks., 1681.
Ann Dunch, a child, quadrilateral plate, Little Wittenham, Berks., 1683.
Edw. Turpin and wife, Bassingbourn, Cambs., 1683.
Dorothy Williams, Pimperne, Dorset., 1694.
John Price (naval officer) and wife, Leigh, Essex, 1709.
John Massie and family, St Peter's, Leeds, Yorks., 1709.
Thos. Lund (mayor), Newark, Notts., 1715.
Philadelphia Greenwood, quadrilateral plate, St Mary Cray, Kent, 1747.
Benj. Greenwood, St Mary Cray, Kent, 1773.

XII

Special Types: Heart Brasses.

Some others which differ in various ways from the two types described in the text are included below:

Anne Muston, Saltwood, Kent, 1496.
Unknown, Fakenham, Norfolk, c. 1500.
Unknown, Higham Ferrers, Northants., c. 1510.
Crystofer Tonson and wife, Melton Mowbray, Leics., 1543.
Thos. Hodges, Wedmore, Somerset, c. 1630.
Grace White, Ludham, Norfolk, 1633.

In the Saltwood and Wedmore brasses it is distinctly stated that only the bowel or heart is buried there.

Sir Thos. Hodges was killed at the siege of Antwerp 1583, and asked that his body should be buried there and his heart sent home to his wife.

At Saltwood an angel, rising from a cloud, holds a heart.

At Fakenham there are four double hearts inscribed "Jhu, mercy," "Lady, help." It is evidently to the memory of a husband and wife whose names are unknown.

Shroud Brasses.

John Brigge, Sall, Norfolk, 1454.
John Manfield, Taplow, Bucks., 1455.
Thos. Pethyn, priest, Lytchett Maltravers, Dorset, c. 1470.
Man and wife, Sedgefield, Durham, c. 1470.
Thos. Fleming, New Coll., Oxford, 1472.
A Priest, Stifford, Essex, c. 1480.
Man and wife, Baldock, Herts., c. 1480.
Tomesina Tendryng, Yoxford, Suff., 1485.
Thos. Spryng and wife, Lavenham, Staff., 1486.
Several at Hitchin, Herts., 1480-1490.
A Man and wife, Sawston, Cambs., c. 1500.
A Lady, Gt. Fransham, Norfolk, c. 1500.
Ralph Hamsterley, a priest, Oddington, Oxon., c. 1500.
Wm. Gibsson and wife, Watlington, Oxon., 1501.
Thos. Tyard, priest, Bawburgh, Norfolk, 1505.
Joan Strangbon, Childrey, Berks., 1507.
Man and wife, West Molesey, Surrey, c. 1510.
Hen. Scolows and wife, St Michael Coslany, Norwich, 1515.
John Goodryngton, Appleton, Berks., 1518.
Unknown, Wooburn, Bucks., c. 1520.
Unknown and wife, Childrey, Berks., c. 1520.
John Claimond, Corpus Christi, Oxford, c. 1530.
Eliz. Rok, Penn, Bucks., 1540.
Wm. Fyssher, master, Wigston's Hospital, Leicester, 1543.
Lucas Goodyere, Aldenham, Herts., 1547.
Hugh Brystowe, priest, Waddesdon, Bucks., 1548.
Unknown, Chicheley, Bucks., 1560.
A Lady, Leigh, Kent, c. 1580.

APPENDIX 143

Thos. Nele, Cassington, Oxon., 1590.
John Maunsell, Haversham, Bucks., 1605.
Eliz. Popeley, Birstall, Yorks., 1632.
Lady Mary Howard, West Firle, Sussex, 1638.
Wives of Clere Talbot, Dunston, Norfolk, 1649.
Philipp Tenison, S.T.P., Bawburgh, Norfolk, 1660.

Skeleton Brasses.

Rich. Notfelde, St John's, Margate, Kent, c. 1446.
Thos. Childes, St Lawrence, Norwich, 1452.
Three Skeletons, Weybridge, Surrey, c. 1520.
A Skeleton in shroud, Hildersham, Cambs., c. 1530.
Barbara Ferrer, St Michael-at-Plea, Norwich, 1588.

XIII

Later Foreign Brasses.

Roger Thornton and wife, All Saints, Newcastle-on-Tyne, 1429.
Thos. Pownder and wife, St Mary Quay, Ipswich, 1525.
Margaret Hornebolt, Fulham, Middlesex, 1529.
Andrew Evyngar and wife, All Hallows, Barking, c. 1535.
Duncan Liddell, M.D., St Nicholas, Aberdeen, 1613.

The Newcastle brass measures 7 ft. × 4 ft. 4 in. The civilian and his wife completely fill the spaces under the canopy, so that no background is necessary. There are saints and angels in the niches, and each soul is shown borne aloft by angels and again in God the Father's arms.

Below the main figures are seven sons and seven daughters, each under a canopy. It is probably North German work. There are no less than 92 figures altogether.

The brasses to Pownder and Evyngar are both Flemish, and somewhat similar in size and design. These sixteenth century brasses are much smaller than those of the fourteenth century.

Pownder's has a marginal inscription and an outer border of foliage. The merchant and his wife stand beneath a Renaissance canopy. Two sons and six daughters kneel at his feet.

Evyngar's brass is very similar, but there is no border, and the inscription is at the foot instead of round the edge.

Margaret Hornebolt was the wife of a Flemish painter from Ghent. The brass is lozenge-shaped and shows her as a demi-figure in a shroud with angels supporting the inscription. The Scotch brass was engraved in Antwerp by the instruction of Liddel's brother John. It is just over 5 ft. high. There is a marginal inscription, and half the space within it is also filled with inscription.

The doctor is shown above this seated at table, with books, writing materials, etc. around him. It reminds us of the seventeenth century brasses to Airay and Bp. Robinson.

In the Victoria and Albert Museum are two other foreign brasses. The larger is also Flemish, to Sire Louis Corteville and wife, 1504. It was originally in the ruined chapel of the Castle of Corteville, Flanders, thence passed to a shop in Antwerp and thence to the Jermyn Street Museum. Recently it has been set up at South Kensington. It has a fillet of foliage and within that a border inscription. The places of the four Evangelists at the corners are filled by shields; there is no canopy. Above the knight, his crest, helmet and coat-of-arms appear, above his wife, a coat-of-arms is supported by an angel. The heads of both rest on embroidered cushions, and the background is covered with a design of foliage.

The armour of the knight, though similar to that of the same date in England, shows several minor variations, which should be studied by those interested in the subject.

The other brass is much smaller and is of German origin. It

APPENDIX 145

is to Henry Oskens, canon, from Nippes, near Cologne, 1535. It is beautifully engraved. Oskens kneels in adoration to the Virgin. Rays of light stream from behind her. These are coloured red, the rest of the engraving being mostly filled in with black wax or some similar substance. This, coupled with the fineness of the engraving, renders it impossible to take a good rubbing.

This completes the list of foreign brasses in England. It will be noticed that the majority of the earlier ones are German, and the later Flemish.

One or two other brasses show traces of foreign (probably French) work, but to them reference has already been made. Thus the knights at Chartham and Minster, and the priest at Horsmonden were probably engraved by French craftsmen. Since, however, only five or six late brasses still survive in France, it is impossible to say for certain.

XIV

Canopies: a selection.

Fourteenth Century.

Several at Cobham.
Hereford Cathedral, canopy and super-canopy, 1360.
Fletching, Sussex, double with centre shaft, c. 1380.
Letheringham, Suffolk, single, 1389.
Fulbourn, Cambs., single, 1391.
Stoke Fleming, Devon, double (peculiar), 1391.
Westminster Abbey, single, 1397.
Boston, Lincs., double triple, with super-canopy and saints in shafts, 1398.

Fifteenth Century.

Balsham, Cambs., triple, 1401.
Bottesford, Leics., triple, 1404.

146 BRASSES

Burgate, Suffolk, double, 1409.
Kidderminster, Worcs., triple, 1415.
Lynwode, Lincs., double with super-canopy, 1419.
Trotton, Sussex, double with super-canopy, 1419.
Horley, Surrey, single, c. 1420.
Warbleton, Sussex, single, 1436.
Okeover, Staffs., triple, 1447.
Hildersham, Cambs., single, 1466.
Enfield, Middlesex, triple, c. 1470.
Thornton, Bucks., quadruple, 1472.
Isleham, Cambs., triple, 1484.
Westminster Abbey, triple, 1498.

Sixteenth Century.

Two, Ardingley, Sussex, double, engraved c. 1500 and 1504.
Cobham, double, 1506.
Hunstanton, triple with figures in side shafts, etc., 1506.
Wyvenhoe, Essex, triple, 1507.
Hillingdon, Middlesex, double, 1509.
Northleach, Glos., double, 1526.
Faversham, Kent, double, 1533.
Ashbourn, Derbs., double, 1538.

Fifteenth century brackets.

A Lady, Southfleet, Kent, 1414.
A Priest, Cotterstock, Northants. (with canopy), 1420.
A Priest, Cobham, Kent (with triple canopy), c. 1420.
John Bloxham and Jn. Whytton, priests, Merton Coll., Oxford, c. 1420.
Wm. Harwedon and wife, Gt. Harrowden, Northants., 1433.
Prior Langley, St Lawrence, Norwich, 1437.
Thos. Roose and wife, Sall, Norfolk, 1440.
Civilian and wife, St George, Colegate, Norwich, 1472.

APPENDIX 147

Plain Crosses.

Unknown, Grainthorpe, Lincs., c. 1380.
Thos. Chichele and wife, Higham Ferrers, Northants., 1400.
Sir Roger Cheyne, Cassington, Oxon., 1414.
Margaret Oliver, Beddington, Surrey, 1425.
Rich. Tooner (priest), Broadwater, Sussex, 1445.
Joan Brokes, Peperharrow, Surrey, 1487.
Unknown, Royston, Herts., c. 1500.
Rich. Pendilton, Eversley, Hants., 1502.
Herward Bwllayen, Hever, Kent, c. 1520.
Alice Wyrley, Floore, Northants., 1537.

Octofoil Crosses with the deceased in the centre.

Nich. Aumberdene (fishmonger), Taplow, Bucks., 1350.
Wm. de Herlestone (priest), Sparsholt, Bucks., c. 1360.
A priest in civil dress, Merton College, Oxford, 1372.
A priest in cope, Hereford Cathedral, c. 1390.
John Lumbarde (priest), Stone, Kent, 1408.

BIBLIOGRAPHY

General.

Manual for the Study of Monumental Brasses (Oxon., 1848).
Boutell's Monumental Brasses (Lond., 1849).
Haines. Manual of Monumental Brasses (1861).
Waller's Series of Monumental Brasses (Lond. and Oxford, 1863).
H. W. Macklin. Monumental Brasses (1890).
H. W. Macklin. The Brasses of England (Methuen, 1907).

Counties.

Cotman's Brasses of Norfolk (1813-16).
    Second Edition (Lond. 1839).
Brasses in Cambridge. Camden Society (1846).
F. Hudson. Brasses of Northamptonshire (1853).
G. Kite. Brasses of Wiltshire (1860).
E. H. W. Dunken. Brasses of Cornwall (1882).
C. T. Davis. Brasses in Worcestershire and Herefordshire (1884).
W. D. Belcher. Kentish Brasses (1888).
Rev. E. Farrar. Brasses of Norfolk (1890).
Ja. Thornely. Brasses in Lancs. and Cheshire (1893, Hull).
Grace Isherwood. Brasses in the Bedfordshire Churches.
W. F. Andrews. Brasses in Herefordshire (1903).
The Transactions of the Monumental Brass Society, London, since 1886.

Foreign.

Monumental Brasses and Incised Slabs in Belgium (1849).
Books of Facsimiles of Monumental Brasses of the Continent of Europe by Rev. W. F. Creeny, 1884.

INDEX

This index is meant as a guide to the most interesting brasses in each county. At the same time, though it includes all mentioned in this manual, it does not profess to be exhaustive. Where there are several brasses at one church the author has often only given one or two, knowing that when there the *brass-rubber* will look round for others.

BEDFORDSHIRE—
Ampthill, *1450*, 119
Aspley Guise, c. *1410*, 124
Bedford, *1663*, 140
Bromham, c. *1435*, 52, 117; *1535*, 52
Cople, c. *1410*, 24; *1544*, 136; *1556*, 136
Dean, *1501*, 125
Dunstable, *1450*, 119
Elstow, c. *1525*, 130
Eyworth, *1624*, 138
Holwell, *1515*, 34
Luton, *1513*, 134
Marston Mortayne, *1451*, 118
Shillington, *1400*, 125
Wimington, *1391*, 14, 115
Yelden, *1434*, 123

BERKSHIRE—
Abingdon, *1501*, 128
Appleton, *1518*, 142
Ashbury, c. *1360*, 115
Binfield, *1558*, 131
Blewbury, *1496*, 123; *1548*, 136
Bray, *1378*, 12, 92, 113; *1475*, 126
Childrey, *1507*, 77, 142; *1520*, 82, 142; *1529*, 128

BERKSHIRE (*cont.*)
Cookham, *1503*, 135; *1577*, 132
Hanney, West, c. *1370*, 122
Reading, St Lawrence, *1538*, 131
Shottesbrook, c. *1370*, 115
Sparsholt, c. *1360*, 122
Windsor, St Geo. Chapel, *1475*, 27; *1522*, 77, 98, 125; *1630*, 75; *1633*, 75
Wittenham, Little, c. *1585*, 68, 91, 137; *1683*, 141

BUCKINGHAMSHIRE—
Caversfield, *1538*, 80
Chalfont St Peter, *1545*, 51, 123
Chenies, *1469*, 121
Chesham Bois, *1520*, 135
Chicheley, *1558*, 62; *1560*, 142
Crawley, North, *1589*, 138
Denham, c. *1440*, 48, 129; *1540*, 48, 130; *1561* (lost), 68
Dinton, *1628*, 139
Drayton Beauchamp, *1368*, 113
Emberton, *1410*, 122
Eton College, *1489*, 125; *1503*, 125; *1522*, 126; *1535*, 123; *1540*, 38

150 INDEX

BUCKINGHAMSHIRE (*cont.*)
Halton, *1553*, 62
Hampden, Great, *1553*, 136
Haversham, *1605*, 142
Hedgerley, *1540*, 131
Marsworth, *1681*, 141
Milton Keynes, *1427*, 123
Penn, *1540*, 142; *1638*, 139
Quainton, *1360*, 116
Shalston, *1540*, 130
Sparsholt, *c. 1360*, 147
Taplow, *1350*, 97, 147; *1455*, 142; *1540*, 131
Thornton, *1472*, 27, 120, 146
Tingewick, *1608*, 70
Turweston, *1450*, 123
Twyford, *1550*, 136
Waddesdon, *1548*, 60, 142
Winchendon, Over, *1515*, 130
Wooburn, *1519*, 126; *c. 1520*, 77, 142

CAMBRIDGESHIRE—
Balsham, *1401*, 36, 90, 125, 145; *1462*, 37, 89, 126, 149
Barton, *c. 1593*, 137
Bassingbourn, *1683*, 141
Burwell, *1542*, 31, 44, 78, 130
Cambridge,
  Christ's College, *c. 1535*, 128
  King's College, *1496*, 39, 127; *1528*, 125; *1558*, 61, 125
  Queens' College, *c. 1535*, 128
  St John's College, *1410*, 127
  Trinity Hall *1517*, 126; *c. 1530*, 127
  St Bene't's, *1432*, 39
  St Mary-the-Less, *c. 1480*, 127
Croxton, *1589*, 138

CAMBRIDGESHIRE (*cont.*)
Ely Cathedral, *1554*, 42, 61, 129; *1614*, 138
Fulbourn, *1391*, 125, 145; *1477*, 123
Girton, *1492*, 126
Hildersham, *1379*, 95, 96; *1466*, 25, 119, 146; *1530*, 142
Hinxton, *1416*, 117
Horseheath, *1382*, 113
Impington, *1505*, 134
Isleham, *1451*, 118; *1484*, 120, 146
March, *1517*, 77, 134
Milton, *1553*, 62; *1660*, 140
Sawston, *1500*, 142
Shelford, Great, *1418*, 126
Shelford, Little, *c. 1480*, 127
Stow-cum-Quy, *c. 1465*, 119
Swaffham, *1638*, 139
Trumpington, *1289*, 3, 112
Westley Waterless, *c. 1325*, 4, 7, 112
Wilbraham, Little, *1521*, 38
Wood Ditton, *1393*, 114

CHESHIRE—
Chester, Holy Trinity, *1530*, 116; *1545*, 131
Macclesfield, *1460*, 119
Wilmslow, *1506*, 79

CORNWALL—
Callington, *c. 1465*, 120
Cardynham, *c. 1400*, 124
Quethiock, *1631*, 139
St Columb Major, *c. 1630*, 139
St Michael Penkevil, *1515*, 128; *c. 1640*, 139
Stratton, *1561*, 137

INDEX

CUMBERLAND—
  Carlisle Cathedral, *1496*, 128; *1616*, 69, 70, 98
  Edenhall, *1458*, 27

DERBYSHIRE—
  Ashbourn, *1538*, 146
  Chesterfield, *1529*, 134
  Dronfield, *1399*, 123
  Etwall, *1512*, 77
  Hathersage, *1463*, 119
  Kedlestone, *1496*, 133
  Morley, *1470*, 27, 77, 120
  Norbury, *1538*, 136
  Tideswell, *1483*, 122

DEVONSHIRE—
  Chittlehampton, *1480*, 121
  Clovelly, *1655*, 140
  Dartmouth, *1408*, 116
  Exeter Cathedral, *1403*, 126; *1409*, 116
  Haccombe, *1586*, 137; *1656*, 140
  Stoke Fleming, *1391*, 115, 145
  Stoke-in-Teignmouth, *c. 1370*, 121

DORSETSHIRE—
  Evershot, *1524*, 123
  Knowle, *1572*, 137
  Lytchett Maltravers, *c. 1470*, 142
  Milton Abbey, *1565*, 56, 136
  Pimperne, *1694*, 141
  Wimborne Minster, *c. 1440*, 43

DURHAM—
  Billingham, *1480*, 125
  Sedgefield, *c. 1470*, 142

ESSEX—
  Arkesden, *1440*, 118
  Aveley, *1370*, 84, 113
  Barking, *c. 1480*, 127; *1596*, 138
  Bocking, *1420*, 117
  Bowers Gifford, *1348*, 10
  Chigwell, *1631*, 70, 72, 74
  Chrishall, *c. 1370*, 113
  Dagenham, *1479*, 28, 29, 30, 121, 130
  Easton, Little, *c. 1420*, 122; *1483*, 27, 116
  Gosfield, *1439*, 24
  Halstead, *1409*, 116
  Harlow, *1636*, 139
  Horkesley, Little, *1412*, 17, 116
  Ingrave, *c. 1500*, 134
  Laindon, *c. 1480*, 123; *c. 1510*, 123
  Latton, *1467*, 120; *c. 1485*, 133
  Leigh, *1709*, 141
  Pebmarsh, *c. 1320*, 4, 112
  Sandon, *c. 1580*, 138
  Shopland, *1371*, 113
  Stifford, *c. 1480*, 142
  Tiltey Abbey, *1562*; 137
  Tolleshunt Darcy, *c. 1540*, 131
  Upminster, *1455*, 120; *c. 1540*, 131; *1545*, 130
  Wendensloft, *c. 1470*, 130
  Wimbish, *1347*, 10, 97
  Wyvenhoe, *1507*, 133, 134, 146; *1537*, 135

GLOUCESTERSHIRE—
  Bristol,
    St John, *1478*, 121
    St Mary Redcliff, *1439*, 119; *1475*, 27; *c. 1480*, 122
    St Peter, *1461*, 123

GLOUCESTERSHIRE (*cont.*)
Bristol,
  Temple Church, *1396*, 115;
  c *1460*, 133
Campden, Chipping, *1401*, 20;
  1467, 121
Cheltenham, *1513*, 135
Cirencester, *1440*, 119; *1462*,
  25, 119; c. *1480*, 124
Deerhurst, *1400*, 22, 23, 119
Gloucester, St Mary de Crypt,
  1529, 130
Minchinhampton, c. *1510*, 130
Newland, c. *1448*, 19, 118
Northleach, c. *1400*, 118;
  1458, 121; c. *1530*, 124;
  1526, 136, 146
Quinton, c. *1430*, 129
Wootton-under-Edge, *1392*, 114

HAMPSHIRE—
Eversley, *1502*, 94, 147
Odiham, c. *1540*, 131; *1636*,
  135
Ringwood, *1416*, 126
Somborne, King's, c. *1380*, 14,
  115
Stoke Charity, *1482*, 78
Thruxton, c. *1425*, 117
Wallop, Nether, *1436*, 129
Winchester College, *1413*, 125;
  1548, 36, 61, 127, 131
  St Cross, *1382*, 125
Isle of Wight,
  Arreton, *1430*, 118
  Calbourne, c. *1380*, 113; *1652*,
    75
  Freshwater, *1370*, 113
  Shorwell, *1518*, 124

HEREFORDSHIRE—
Hereford Cathedral, *1360*, 128,

HEREFORDSHIRE (*cont.*)
  145; c. *1390*, 147; *1434*,
  126; *1435*, 117; *1524*, 78,
  91; *1529*, 91; *1536*, 126
Ledbury, c. *1410*, 127
Marden, *1614*, 66

HERTFORDSHIRE—
Aldbury, *1546*, 135
Aldenham, *1547*, 142
Ashridge House, *1395*, 122
Baldock, c. *1480*, 142
Bayford, c. *1545*, 132
Bennington, c. *1450*, 37
Berkhampstead, Great, *1356*,
  12, 115; *1365*, 113
Broxbourne, *1473*, 27, 56; *1531*,
  134
Buckland, *1478*, 126
Clothall, *1519*, 123; *1541*, 127;
  1602, 138
Digswell, *1415*, 19
Hitchin, *1480-90*, 142; *1498*,
  37, 126
Knebsworth, *1414*, 126; *1582*,
  137
Letchworth, *1475*, 123
Mimms, North, c. *1360*, 84, 122
Royston, c. *1500*, 147
St Albans,
  Abbey, *1360*, 84, 128; *1401*,
    128; *1411*, 118; c. *1450*,
    129; c. *1470*, 129; *1480*,
    27, 120; *1519*, 136; *1521*,
    130
  St Michael, c. *1380*, 113
Sawbridgeworth, *1433*, 117; c.
  1600, 137
Standon, *1477*, 121
Watford, *1415*, 119
Watton, *1361*, 113; c. *1370*, 129
Willian, *1446*, 123

INDEX 153

KENT
  Addington, *1409*, 116; *1470*, 25, 120
  Ash-next-Sandwich, *c. 1460*, 120; *1602*, 137
  Aylesford, *1545*, 132
  Beckenham, *1552*, 136
  Borden, *1490*, 125
  Boughton-under-Blean, *1587*, 64
  Boxley, *1451*, 127
  Brabourn, *1434*, 117
  Canterbury,
    St George, *1438*, 126
    St Margaret, *1470*, 121
    St Martin, *1591*, 137
  Chart, Great, *c. 1470*, 121; *1680*, 75, 140
  Chartham, *1306*, 3, 112, 145; *1456*, 126
  Chelsfield, *1417*, 96
  Chevening, *1596*, 138
  Cliffe, *1652*, 140
  Cobham, *1320*, 7, 88; *1354*, 113; *c. 1365*, 12, 99, 113; *1367*, 113; *1375*, 13, 114; *c. 1380*, 114; *1395*, 13, 77, 88, 115; *1405*, 116; *1407*, 77, 90, 116; *1420*, 146; *1433*, 19; *1506*, 146; *1529*, 134
  Cranbrook, *c. 1520*, 135
  Cray, St Mary, *1747, 1773*, 76, 140
  Dartford, *1402*, 118; *1454*, 120
  Deal, Upper, *1606*, 135
  Dover, St James, *c. 1590*, 138
  Downe, *1596*, 138
  Eastry, *1590*, 64
  Faversham, *1533*, 133, 136, 146
  Graveney, *c. 1370*, 115; *1436*, 119

KENT (*cont.*)
  Halstow, High, *1618*, 38
  Hardres, Upper, *1405*, 91, 92, 93, 127
  Herne, *c. 1420*, 118; *c. 1450*, 127; *1470*, 120
  Hever, *1419*, 19; *c. 1520*, 147; *1538*, 116, 134
  Hoo St Werburgh, *1412*, 122
  Horsmonden, *c. 1340*, 122, 145
  Kemsing, *c. 1320*, 32, 112
  Leigh, *c. 1580*, 142
  Lydd, *1420*, 127
  Maling, East, *1522*, 125
  Margate, St John, *1431*, 20; *1433*, 80; *1446*, 142; *1582*, 133; *1615*, 82
  Mereworth, *1371*, 113
  Minster-in-Sheppey, *c. 1330*, 5, 7, 112, 145
  Monkton-in-Thanet, *c. 1465*, 123
  Northfleet, *1375*, 122
  Otterden, *1408*, 116
  Rochester, St Margaret, *1465*, 50
  Saltwood, *1496*, 141
  Seal, *1395*, 114
  Sheldwich, *1394*, 114
  Shorne, *1519*, 124
  Southfleet, *1414*, 146
  Stone, *1408*, 147
  Sutton, East, *1638*, 71, 72
  Upchurch, *1340*, 115
  Westerham, *1563*, 132; *1567*, 168
  Wickham, East, *c. 1325*, 8, 97, 112
  Woodchurch, *c. 1320*, 8, 97, 112

INDEX

LANCASHIRE—
  Manchester Cathedral, *1458*, 125; *1515*, 129; *1548*, 131
  Middleton, *1650*, 74
  Sefton, *1568*, 137
  Winwick, *1492*, 133; *1527*, 34

LEICESTERSHIRE—
  Barwell, *1659*, 140
  Bosworth, Husbands, *1648*, 140
  Bottesford, *1404*, 77, 126, 145
  Castle Donnington, *1458*, 25, 119
  Leicester, Wigston's Hospital, *1543*, 142
  Melton Mowbray, *1543*, 141
  Stanford-on-Soar, *c. 1400*, 122
  Wanlip, *1393*, 114

LINCOLNSHIRE—
  Althorpe, *c. 1370*, 122
  Bigby, *1642*, 140
  Boston, *1398*, 14, 115, 145; *1657*, 140
  Broughton, *c. 1370*, 113
  Buslingthorpe, *c. 1290*, 3, 79, 112
  Cotes, Great, *1503*, 130
  Croft, *c. 1300*, 112
  Edenham, *c. 1500*, 42, 129
  Grainthorpe, *c. 1380*, 146
  Gunby, *1400*, 115; *1419*, 119
  Horncastle, *1519*, 81
  Irnham, *1390*, 114
  Laughton, *c. 1400*, 115; *1549*, 52
  Lyndewode, *1419*, 118, 145
  Rauceby, *1536*, 37, 126
  Scrivelsby, *1545*, 134
  Spilsby, *1410*, 116
  Stamford, All Saints, *c. 1460*, 121; *1471*, 120; *1508*, 126

LINCOLNSHIRE (*cont.*)
  Tattershall, *1411*, 118; *1455*, 116; *c. 1510*, 126

MIDDLESEX—
  Chelsea, *1555*, 136
  Clerkenwell, St James, *1556*, 42, 61, 129
  Ealing, *c. 1490*, 135
  Edgeware, *1599*, 135
  Enfield, *1470*, 27, 56, 57, 145
  Fulham, *1529*, 143, 144
  Greenford, Great, *c. 1515*, 123
  Hackney, *1521*, 126; *1545*, 134
  Harrow, *c. 1370*, 113; *c. 1390*, 114; *1442*, 126; *c. 1460*, 127
  Hayes, *c. 1370*, 127; *c. 1450*, 118; *1576*, 137
  Hillingdon, *1509*, 133, 134, 146
  Isleworth, *1450*, 118; *1544*, 132; *1561*, 130, 148
  Kilburn, St Mary, *1380*, 129
  London (The City),
    All Hallows', Barking, *1437*, 118; *c. 1510*, 78; *1518*, 135; *c. 1535*, 143, 144; *1546*, 131
    Great St Helen, *1482*, 127; *1510*, 134; *c. 1535*, 135
    St Andrew Undershaft, *1539*, 136
    St Bartholomew-the-Less, *1439*, 119
  Museum, British, *1575*, 132
  Museum, South Kensington, *1504*, 144; *1535*, 58
  Northolt, *1610*, 138
  Pinner, *c. 1580*, 135
  Westminster Abbey, *1395*, 128; *1397*, 128, 145; *1399*, 13, 46, 47, 88, 115, 129; *1437*, 117; *1483*, 120; *1498*, 129,

MIDDLESEX (cont.)
146; *1505*, 134; *1561*, 68, 128; *1661*, 140
Willesdon, *1517*, 126

MONMOUTHSHIRE—
Abergavenny, *1631*, 140

NORFOLK—
Acle, *1627*, 140
Bawburgh, *1505*, 82, 142; *1660*, 82, 143
Beachamwell St Mary, c. *1385*, 122
Bedon, Kirby, c. *1450*, 80
Blickling, *1401*, 116; *1458*, 120
Burg St Margaret, *1608*, 138
Burnham Thorpe, *1420*, 117
Buxton, *1508*, 124
Cley, c. *1520*, 124, 128
Clippesby, *1594*, 137
Creake, North, c. *1500*, 124
— South, *1509*, 130
Dunston, *1649*, 143
Elsing, *1347*, 9, 88
Erpingham, c. *1415*, 117
Fakenham, c. *1500*, 141
Felbrigg, c. *1380*, 113; c. *1382*, 14, 115; *1461*, 17, 18, 116, 117; *1608*, 137
Fransham, Great, *1414*, 117; c. *1500*, 142
Frenze, *1519*, 130
Halvergate, c. *1460*, 129; *1540*, 129, 131
Hedenham, *1502*, 124
Heigham, *1630*, 139
Helbroughton, c. *1450*, 80
Hunstanton, *1506*, 92, 133, 134, 146
Loddon, *1462*, 80
Ludham, *1633*, 141

NORFOLK (cont.)
Lynn, St Margaret, *1349*, 84, 85; *1364*, 84, 85
Mattishall, *1507*, 135
Methwold, *1637*, 113
Narburgh, *1545*, 78
Necton, *1372*, 114
Norwich,
St Ethelred, *1487*, 123
St George, Colgate, *1472*, 146
St Giles, *1499*, 124
St John, Maddermarket,*1440*, 129; *1472*, 121; *1524*, *1525*, 92, 94; *1558*, 92, 94, 131
St Laurence, *1437*, 129, 146; *1452*, 143
St Michael-at-Plea, *1588*, 143
St Michael Coslany, *1515*, 142
St Peter Mancroft, *1568*, 132
Reepham, *1391*, 114
Rougham, *1470*, 120; *1510*, 135
Sall, *1440*, 146; *1454*, 142
Shernborne, *1458*, 119
Sparham, *1490*, 123
Stokesby, *1488*, 133
Surlingham, *1460*, 127; *1513*, 124
Upwell, *1428*, 37, 126; *1435*, 33, 37
Walsham, North, *1519*, 124
Walsingham, Little, c. *1520*, 124
Wiggenhall, *1450*, 80
Witton, *1505*, 130

NORTHAMPTONSHIRE—
Blatherwicke, *1548*, 239
Boddington, Upper, *1627*, 140

156　INDEX

NORTHAMPTONSHIRE (*cont.*)
Brington, Great, *c. 1340*, 127
Cotterstock, *1420*, 126, 146
Easton Neston, *1552*, 136
Fawsley, *1516*, 79
Floore, *1510*, 77; *1537*, 96, 147
Harrowden, Great, *1433*, 117, 146
Higham Ferrers, *1337*, 32, 33, 88, 89, 122, end; *c. 1510*, 141
Kettering, *1631*, 139
Lowick, *1467*, 27
Newton-by-Geddington, *c.1400*, 96
Newton Bromshold, *1426*, 123
Northampton, St Sepulchre, *1640*, 139
Preston Deanery, *1622*, 137
Rothwell, *1361*, 125
Stoke Bruerne, *1625*, 140
Sudborough, *1415*, 33
Tansor, *1440*, 123
Wappenham, *1481*, 121

NORTHUMBERLAND—
Newcastle, *1429*, 143

NOTTINGHAMSHIRE—
Markham, East, *1419*, 19
Newark, *1715*, 141
Ossington, *1551*, 132

OXFORDSHIRE—
Brightwell Baldwin, *1439*, 22, 119
Burford, *1437*, 91
Cassington, *1414*, 146; *1590*, 142
Chalgrove, *1441*, 118
Checkendon, *1404*, 24

OXFORDSHIRE (*cont.*)
Chinnor, *c. 1320*, 8, 97, 112; *1361*, 127; *1385*, 13, 114; *1386*, 114; *1392*, 114; *1410*, 118
Dorchester, *c. 1510*, 46, 130
Ewelme, *1436*, 117; *1518*, 134
Holton, *1599*, 68
Ipsden, *1525*, 77, 133
Lewknor, *1380*, 115
Lillingstone Lovell, *1446*, 80
Lyne, Stoke, *1535*, 142
Northstoke, *1370*, 37
Norton, Chipping, *1451*, 119
Oddington, *c. 1500*, 82, 142
Oxford,
All Souls College, *1510*, 128
Christ Church, *c. 1460*, 121; *1557*, 61, 125
Corpus Christi, *c. 1530*, 142
Magdalen College, *1478*, 127; *1501*, 38; *1515*, 125; *1558*, 38, 61
Merton College, *c. 1310*, 8, 32, 97, 112; *1372*, 147; *c. 1420*, 38, 90, 92, 146; *1471*, 126
New College, *1403*, 126; *1417*, 40, 41, 128; *1427*, 127; *1441*, 127; *1472*, 142; *1494*, 126; *1508*, 38; *c. 1510*, 121; *c. 1525*, 129; *1592*, 137
Queen's College, *1518*, 36, 126; *1616*, 69, 98, 138; *1616* (another), 69, 70
Rotherfield-Grays, *1387*, 114
Shirburn, *1493*, 77
Soulderne, *1508*, 123
Swinbrook, *1510*, 134
Tew, Great, *1410*, 116
Thame, *c. 1460*, 119

INDEX 157

OXFORDSHIRE (cont.)
Waterperry, c. 1370, 114; 1527, 51
Watlington, 1501, 142
Whitchurch, 1456, 123; 1610, 138
Witney, c. 1500, 135

RUTLAND—
Casterton, Little, c. 1410, 116

SHROPSHIRE—
Acton Burnell, 1382, 11, 90, 113
Adderley, 1390, 128
Tong, 1467, 25, 26, 1

SOMERSETSHIRE—
Ilminster, c. 1440, 118; 1618, 137
Shepton Mallet, 1649, 139
Wedmore, c. 1630, 141
Wells Cathedral, 1626, 160
Yeovil, c. 1460, 129

STAFFORDSHIRE—
Clifton Campville, c. 1360, 133
Kinver, 1528, 134
Norbury, c. 1350, 114
Okeover, 1538, 51, 146

SUFFOLK—
Acton, 1302, 3, 112
Ampton, c. 1490, 133
Bildeston, 1599, 66, 67
Brundish, c. 1360, 122; 1560, 136
Burgate, 1409, 145
Bury St Edmunds, 1519, 125
Campsey Ash, 1504, 123
Easton, 1584, 64, 65, 137
Eyke, c. 1430, 119

SUFFOLK (cont.)
Fressingfield, c. 1485, 120
Gazeley, 1530, 124
Gorleston, c. 1320, 4, 112
Hadleigh, c. 1560, 49, 132
Holbrook, 1470, 120
Ipswich, St Mary Quay, 1525, 143
St Mary Tower, c. 1475, 121; 1506, 121
Kenton, 1524, 134
Lavenham, 1486, 142
Letheringham, 1389, 114, 145
Melford, Long, c. 1480, 120
Melton, 1430, 127
Oulton, 1310 (lost), 8
Playford, 1400, 115
Rendham, 1523, 124
Rougham, 1405, 116
Sotterley, c. 1630, 139
Stonham-Aspall, 1606, 69
Wenham, Little, 1514, 133
Wrentham, 1593, 137
Yoxford, 1428, 117; 1485, 142; 1613, 138

SURREY—
Addington, 1540, 134
Albury, 1440, 118
Beddington, 1425, 146; 1432, 118
Betchworth, 1533, 123
Bookham, Great, 1668, 75, 160
Byfleet, 1489, 125
Carshalton, c. 1490, 133
Charlwood, 1553, 136
Cheam, 1370, 115; 1542, 77, 131
Cobham, c. 1500, 78; c. 1550, 131
Cranley, 1503, 78
Crowhurst, 1450, 118

INDEX

SURREY (cont.)
  Croydon, *1512*, 126
  Ewell, *1519*, 134
  Guildford, *1901*, 111
  Horley, *1420*, 19; *1516*, 52, 145
  Horsley, East, *1478*, 40, 128
  Kingston-on-Thames, *1437*, 118
  Lambeth St Mary, *1535*, 135; *1545*, 136
  Lingfield, c. *1370*, 13, 114; *1403*, 116; *1420*, 19; *1469*, 123
  Molesey, West, c. *1510*, 142
  Oxted, *1480*, 120
  Peperharrow, *1487*, 77, 147
  Puttenham, *1431*, 123
  Richmond, *1591*, 137
  Shere, *1412*, 122; c. *1525*, 105
  Stoke d'Abernon, *1277*, 2, 56, 112; *1327*, 4, 5, 112
  Walton-on-Thames, *1587*, 50
  Weybridge, c. *1520*, 143
  Wonersh, *1503*, 135

SUSSEX—
  Amberley, *1424*, 27
  Ardingley, c. *1500*, 56, 58, 133, 135, 146; *1504*, 56, 133, 134, 146; *1634*, 72
  Arundel, *1419*, 125; *1445*, 123; *1463*, 119
  Battle, *1426*, 117; c. *1430*, 123; *1615*, 138
  Bodiam, c. *1360*, 113
  Broadwater, *1432*, 126
  Buxted, *1408*, 97
  Clapham, *1526*, 53, 54, 55, 77
  Cowfold, *1433*, 45, 46, 90, 129

SUSSEX (cont.)
  Etchingham, *1388*, 114
  Firle, West, *1638*, 142
  Fletching, c. *1380*, 113, 145; *1450*, 20
  Horsham, *1411*, 37; c. *1430*, 33
  Hurstmonceaux, *1407*, 116
  Isfield, *1579*, 136
  Ore, c. *1440*, 118
  Pulborough, *1423*, 126; *1452*, 119
  Stopham, c. *1460*, 122; *1614*, 137
  Ticehurst, c. *1370*, 113; *1546*, 52
  Trotton, *1310*, 5, 8, 112; *1419*, 116, 117, 145
  Warbleton, *1436*, 126, 145
  Wiston, *1426*, 117

WARWICKSHIRE—
  Aston, *1545*, 136
  Baginton, *1407*, 15, 116
  Coleshill, *1566*, 138
  Merevale Abbey, *1412*, 116
  Middleton, *1476*, 121
  Warwick, St Mary, *1401*, 15, 16, 115
    St Nicholas, *1424*, 122
  Wellesbourne, *1426*, 117
  Wixford, *1411*, 116

WESTMORLAND—
  Morland, *1562*, 131

WILTSHIRE—
  Dauntsey, *1514*, 134
  Draycott Cerne, *1394*, 114
  Fovant, *1492*, 77, 127
  Mere, *1398*, 114
  Salisbury Cathedral, *1375*, 63, 98, 128; *1578*, 69

INDEX 159

WORCESTERSHIRE—
Alvechurch, *1524*, 134
Blockley, *1488*, 127; c. *1500*, 123
Bredon, *1650*, 140
Kidderminster, *1415*, 117, 145
Strensham, c. *1390*, 114
Tredington, *1427*, 126

YORKSHIRE—
Aldborough, c. *1360*, 113
Aughton, *1466*, 120
Bainton, *1429*, 123
Barton-on-Humber, *1433*, 118
Beeford, *1472*, 37
Borstall, *1632*, 142
Bradfield, *1647*, 139
Brandsburton, *1397*, 114
Burton, Bishop, *1460*, 124
Cottingham, *1383*, 125
Cowthorpe, *1494*, 121
Hamsthwaite, c. *1380*, 115
Harpham, *1445*, 118
Hornby, *1489*, 130
Howden, *1621*, 131
Hutton, Sheriff, *1657*, 140
Kirby Warfe, *1480*, 126
Kirkheaton, *1655*, 74
Leeds St Peter, *1469*, 124; *1709*, 141
Owston, *1409*, 118
Ripley, *1429*, 124
Routh, c. *1410*, 19, 117
Sessay, *1550*, 61, 127, 131
Sprotborough, *1474*, 25, 120
Thornton Watlass, *1669*, 140
Topcliff, *1391*, 84
Wath, *1420*, 119
Wensley, c. *1360*, 84, 86, 122
Winestead, c. *1540*, 132

YORKSHIRE (*cont.*)
York, Minster, *1315*, 8, 40, 112, 128; *1585*, 138; *1595*, 138
All Saints, *1642*, 139
St Crux, *1597*, 138
St Michael Spurriergate, *1466*, 124

IRELAND—
Dublin, St Patrick, *1528*, 98, 125; *1537*, 98, 99, 125

WALES—
Anglesea, Beaumaris, c. *1530*, 115
Denbigh, Llanrwst, *1620*, *1632*, *1658*, *1660*, *1669*, *1671*, 73, 139, 140
Glamorgan, Swansea, c. *1500*, 78, 79
Montgomery, Bettws, *1531*, 123
Pembroke, Haverfordwest, *1654*, 140

SCOTLAND—
Aberdeen, *1613*, 143, 144

THE CONTINENT—
Belgium, Bruges, 15th *cent.*, 83
Brussels, *1398*, 83
Ghent, *14th cent.*, 83
Denmark, Ringstead, engr. c. *1350*, 83, 85
Germany, Lübeck, *1356*, 83, 84
Schwerin, *1347*, 86; *1375*, 86
Stralsund, *1361*, 83, 84
Thorn, *1357*, 83, 84
Verden, *1231*, 1
Switzerland, Constance, 15th *cent.*, 84

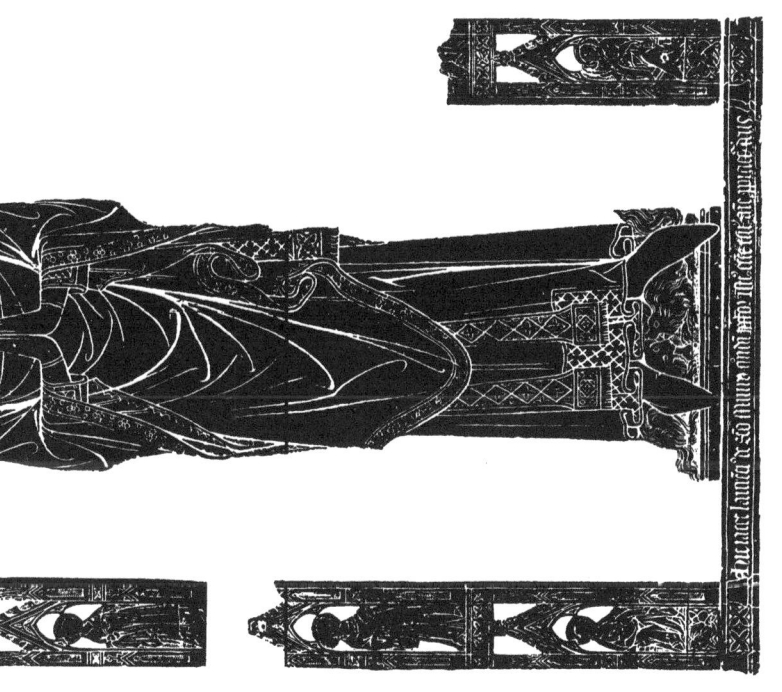

Fig. 13. Laurence de St Maur, 1337, Higham Ferrers, Northants.

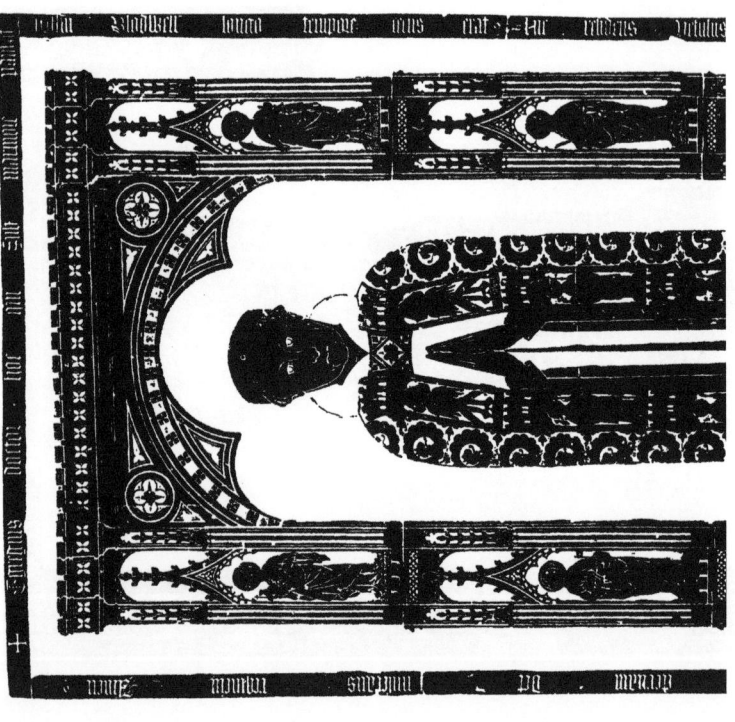

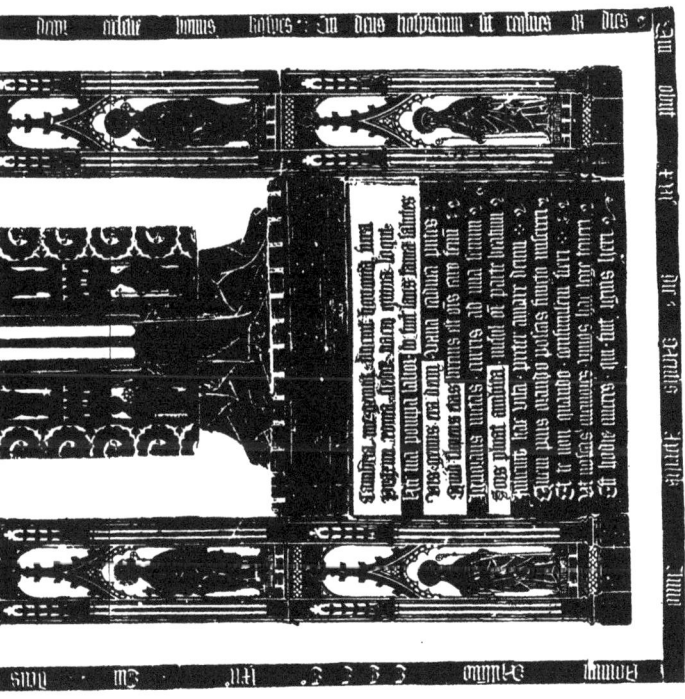

Fig. 14. John Blodwell, Dean of St Asaph, 1462, Balsham, Cambs.

For EU product safety concerns, contact us at Calle de José Abascal, 56–1°,
28003 Madrid, Spain or eugpsr@cambridge.org.

www.ingramcontent.com/pod-product-compliance
Ingram Content Group UK Ltd.
Pitfield, Milton Keynes, MK11 3LW, UK
UKHW041411180426
11947UKWH00007B/58